SO YOU
WANT TO BUY
A PONY?

The Pony Club
Stoneleigh Park
Kenilworth
Warwickshire
CV8 2RW

Website: www.pcuk.org

So You Want to Buy a Pony?
is published by The Pony Club

© 2012 The Pony Club
Text © 2012 Carolyn Henderson
Photographs © 2012 John Henderson
Illustrations © 2012 Maggie Raynor
Cover photograph © 2012 Kit Houghton/The Pony Club

British Library Cataloguing in Publication Data.
A catalogue record for this book is available from the British Library.

ISBN 978-1-907279-14-0

Design and Production: Paul G. Harding

Printed by Halstan Printing Group in Amersham, UK
www.halstan.co.uk

Trade distribution by Kenilworth Press
An imprint of Quiller Publishing Ltd.
Wykey House, Wykey, Shrewsbury, SY4 1JA
Tel: 01939 261616 Fax: 01939 261606
E-mail: info@quillerbooks.com
Website: www.kenilworthpress.co.uk

SO YOU
WANT TO BUY
A PONY?

Carolyn Henderson

Contents

1. Making Plans

First Thoughts

Buying a pony will change your life. It's challenging as well as exciting, but reading this book means you've taken the first essential step—finding out what's involved so that you can make the right decisions. It's aimed particularly at first-time buyers, including those who do not have an equestrian background, but it should also help the more experienced.

Whether you're a young rider and would-be pony owner or a parent who will be paying the bills, remember that a pony will impose more demands than any other animal, because of the time and costs involved. This could affect all members of the family, even those who are not interested in ponies, so will everyone be happy at the prospect of a new addition to it?

You do not have to be rich to own a pony, but you do need to be realistic about what ownership will cost. It is also essential to make sure that you can dedicate the time needed to keep him healthy and happy. Don't just think about the time needed for riding, think about all the other jobs—including the not so exciting ones, such as picking up droppings in the field!

Buying a pony is a commitment for parents as well as children.

Adults must appreciate that children must have practical as well as financial support, seven days a week. You cannot leave a pony in a field for a day without carrying out routine checks and care, or making sure that this is done by someone appropriate and reliable, just because something unexpected comes up. Providing support may involve you in everything from driving to the yard where the pony is kept to helping to carry heavy bales of bedding or bags of feed.

The other factor to consider is your level of experience and whether or not you have adequate back-up. If you have not already done so, join a Branch of The Pony Club, which will give you instant access to advice, instruction and a great social network. Everyone has to start somewhere and it is better to be a novice owner with a good support network than someone who may have owned a pony for a long time but lacks knowledge.

You do not have to own a pony to join The Pony Club, so you can do so even if owning a pony is still a long-term ambition. Wherever you live, you will find a local Branch.

A pony is usually accepted as being an animal up to 14.2hh or 148cm and under—see Chapter 3 for more information—but taller riders may need something bigger. Therefore, although this book is mainly about ponies, there are some references to horses. Unless otherwise specified, the advice given applies to both.

Ready or Not?

Thoughts for riders

If you are a would-be pony owner, be honest about whether you are ready to go ahead. Are your riding skills at a suitable level and do you have the basic practical skills needed?

Most people learn to ride at a riding school, where they should also get the chance to learn basic horse and pony care. There are also lots of magazines, DVDs and internet sites bursting with information, but although many of these can be valuable, you must also have hands-on experience. As a

Opposite: Do your riding skills match your idea of the kind of pony you hope to buy?

guideline, before you think about buying a pony, you should be proficient in the following areas:

- Be able to control a pony suitable for your ability at walk, trot and canter and jump a small fence, in a safe area and under supervision.
- Be able to ride in the open and control your pony in all three gaits. If your riding school is in an appropriate location, hopefully you will also be able to hack out with a qualified escort.
- Be happy and confident handling a well-behaved pony, including catching, leading, tacking-up and untacking and grooming.
- Know what a pony will dislike or may be frightened by, such as sudden loud noises or inconsiderate handling.
- Understand the basics of pony care, such as why it is important not to let ponies get fat and why they need routine preventive care such as worming and vaccination.

Thoughts for parents

Inevitably, parents make the decision on whether or not to buy a pony, as they are the ones who pay the bills and provide practical support. There are several issues to consider, but the first must be whether or not the rider is ready. Talking through the section above will give you some idea, but do not allow yourself to be persuaded without talking to an instructor who knows your child well enough to advise you.

It is important that at least one adult in the family should know how to handle a pony and be confident in catching, leading, picking up feet and other basic tasks. If you do not have this experience, ask your child's instructor to arrange a practical lesson or two for you.

TIP

Riding your own pony is much more challenging than riding one owned by a riding school. Riding school ponies are used to a strict work routine and usually know more about their job than their riders do. While you will need plenty of guidance to ride and look after your own pony, you will also have to think for yourself, because there will not always be someone to tell you where to go and what to do. With the right pony and the right help, you will make rapid progress, but you should be confident enough to ride and handle different types of pony before looking for one of your own.

If discussions encourage you to go ahead, the next step is to work out costs. These will vary depending on the value of the pony, where and how you keep him and what you do with him, but there are constants. One is that the purchase price is just a starting point.

Costing it out

Below is a list of regular costs which every owner will incur. Detailed advice on how to look after a pony can be found in other Pony Club publications, though throughout this book, you will find basic information which will help make things clearer.

- Accommodation for your pony, usually called livery. This is a term which goes back to the days when livery yards kept horses for hire.
- Feed and, if he is stabled for part of the time, bedding. Whatever management system you choose—and the options are explained in the next section—a pony will need extra fuel in the winter when there is little or no nutritional value in grass. In many cases, this need will be supplied by good quality hay and a broad spectrum vitamin and mineral supplement that makes up for any deficiencies in his diet. In certain circumstances, such as when a pony is working extra hard, he may need his diet supplementing with suitably formulated food in the form of cubes or mix, usually called hard feed.

Farriery costs must be counted in to your regular expenditure.

- Some ponies may need to be on restricted grazing when the food value of grass is at its peak, not just to prevent them becoming overweight but to minimise the risk of a crippling foot condition called laminitis. Unfortunately this doesn't mean they are extra cheap to keep, as they will need hay or other low calorie forage as a replacement for rich grass.
- Tack (a term which covers bridles, saddles, headcollars and so on) and other equipment. Things you will need range from the obvious, such as a saddle, bridle and headcollar to grooming kit, winter rugs, mucking-out tools and first aid equipment.
- Farriery—trimming and shoeing. All ponies—even those who go unshod—need their feet trimming roughly every six weeks and most, though not all, will wear shoes.
- Insurance—public liability insurance is essential and is part of The Pony Club membership package. It is also recommended that you take out insurance against veterinary fees, as explained in Chapter 7.
- Routine preventive care—vaccination, worming and dental care. All equines need basic protection against tetanus and equine influenza. They also need worming regularly, to keep them and their grazing in good

Tack is another major investment.

health. A good yard will have a worming programme in place that has been devised to protect the animals who live there.

- Regular dental care is essential for all equines, including those who aren't ridden. Their teeth can develop sharp edges which, if left unattended, will interfere with the animal's ability to eat and cause him discomfort when wearing a bit.
- Time and transport costs—practical support will be as essential as paying the bills. If you are responsible for the pony's daily care, you must be prepared to visit him twice a day to make essential checks and carry out necessary tasks, or make sure that someone suitably experienced and reliable is doing so.
- Lessons—because you never stop learning. You will need help to build a relationship with your new pony and a big part of that will be learning to ride him effectively and safely. Even Olympic riders have help from trainers and coaches.
- Transport for rallies, shows and so on. Most people eventually buy their own horsebox or trailer, but you can also hire a professional, licensed transporter. Hiring is often a cost-effective way of travelling if several people on the same yard get together.

Give it a try

If you buy a car and decide after a month that it is not the one you want, it is easy to sell it and start again. A pony is not a disposable object. There are times when it is best for everyone, including the pony, to find him a new home, such as when his rider outgrows him. However, no one should buy a pony with the attitude that if the responsibilities are too demanding, he can be got rid of just as easily.

In some ways it might seem like a vicious circle. How can you know what is involved until you actually do it?

Rather than trusting to luck, get as much practical experience as possible. Many riding schools run 'own a pony' courses during school holidays, where parents and children can learn what pony ownership involves. It makes life easier and safer if as many family members as possible are confident in handling a pony, even if only one person will be riding him.

Talk to other people about how they manage. Most owners love talking about their ponies and you will find that the pleasure they get from them outweighs the compromises or even sacrifices they make to keep them.

Buy, Loan or Share?

Buying a pony is not the only option. In some cases, loaning or sharing one might work well, though neither option should be thought of as involving less responsibility. A pony relies on you whether or not you are his legal owner.

You might think that loaning or sharing means half the headaches and responsibilities but none of the rights, and that you would be better off buying and sharing a pony in partnership with a friend in similar circumstances. That sounds fine in theory but, in practice, it can be a nightmare if things go wrong and an arrangement has to be terminated.

However, sharing a pony can be a good option in some cases, especially for those who cannot commit the time or money required for full-time ownership. The usual arrangement is that the sharer is responsible for a percentage of the costs and work in return for being able to ride the pony. The advantages are self-explanatory, but you have to accept that you would not have the same freedom as you would if you owned a pony.

You have to decide whether you are going to buy, loan or share a pony.

There are many reasons why a pony may be offered on loan. A common scenario is that although one child in a family has outgrown a pony, a younger brother or sister will one day be ready to take over. Rather than sell the pony, his owners may prefer to put him on loan for a set period so that they can have him back when his next rider is ready for him.

You may also find families who have become so fond of a pony that selling him seems unthinkable. However, you might find that, once his owners have got used to his absence, they decide that it would be better to sell after all. Depending on your circumstances, this may or may not be good news.

Charities such as World Horse Welfare and the Blue Cross often have ponies who have been signed over to them for various reasons and, after assessment, are placed on loan to suitable borrowers and checked at regular intervals. As long as you accept that you have to demonstrate that you will be a suitable borrower, that it may take some time for a suitable pony to become available and that he will never belong to you, this can work well—and you also have the satisfaction of helping these charities' valuable work.

The need for agreements

Both loan and share arrangements only work if detailed agreements are made. They should be made in writing and signed by both parties so that there is no risk of misunderstanding and some people prefer to have a loan/share agreement drawn up by a solicitor. If you do this, make sure the solicitor has specialist equestrian knowledge.

Points to think about include:

- The timescale of the agreement and the amount of notice that should be given on each side. A sensible owner will retain the right to end an agreement immediately if there are any justified concerns.
- Where will the pony be kept?
- How will costs be divided and who will be responsible for what? A common scenario when sharing is that day-to-day costs such as livery, preventive care, farriery and, perhaps, insurance are split while the owner remains responsible for capital costs, i.e. buying major items of equipment.
- How long does the agreement stay in place if the pony is ill or injured and cannot be ridden?
- What is the pony to be used for and are there some activities not allowed?
- With a share agreement, you also need to consider how riding time—including, if appropriate, the chance to compete—is allocated.

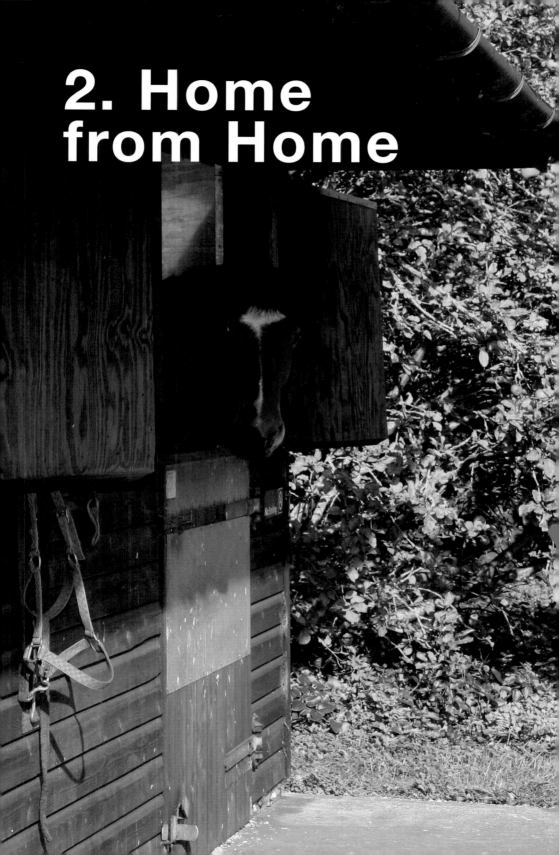

2. Home from Home

Somewhere to Live

Before you look for a pony, you must find somewhere to keep him. Doing it the other way round means you are under pressure and may have to settle for second best. You cannot assume that the sellers will be able and willing to keep him until you find accommodation—and if they are, expect to pay a suitable boarding fee.

Nor is it fair to use a second-rate yard as a stopgap while you shop around for something better. Moving homes is unsettling for the quietest pony and to do it twice in quick succession will put him under further stress. Find a yard you are happy with first and, if necessary, be prepared to pay a retainer until you find your pony.

If you are lucky enough to have facilities for keeping horses or ponies at home, you may think you do not need to worry about the above considerations. However, if this is your first experience of owning a pony, you and he will be much better starting off on a good professional yard. Here, you will have experienced and knowledgeable back-up from the owner or manager and the moral support and company of other owners.

You also have to take into account the fact that equines are herd animals and a lone pony will need a suitable companion. Although it should be easy to find one, even a retired companion who does not need to be ridden will require the same level of care as your pony, which will double costs such as winter forage, hoof trimming, vaccination, worming and dental care.

It is important to find a home for your pony where he—and you—will be happy.

Lifestyle choices

Horses and ponies, like people, need to be happy in their lifestyles. The best way to keep a pony happy is to keep him, as far as possible, as nature intended, remembering that he is no longer a wild animal who has to spend 15 hours or more out of every 24 covering long distances in search of forage, whilst avoiding predators. He certainly retains his natural instincts, but he is a domesticated animal with a job to do—so while his lifestyle should be as natural as possible, there are limits to how far it can or should replicate that of the wild horse.

At one time, there was a huge backlash from some quarters against everything from stabling horses to shoeing them. As a result, many caring owners were made to feel guilty. Fortunately, most people now try to take a balanced view and give their horses and ponies a balanced lifestyle that prioritises their natural requirements but also keeps them healthy and safe.

It is essential that horses and ponies have plenty of time turned out to graze, unless your vet recommends otherwise. However, it may also be necessary to stable them at times and as long as their environment is appropriate, most are perfectly happy. In many cases, a combined management regime of being (usually) out in the day and in at night may be the best choice.

Whether or not it is best to shoe a pony depends on the quality of his feet, the work he is going to do and the surfaces he is going to be ridden on. Every case should be looked at on an individual basis and discussed with your farrier and, if necessary, your vet.

Livery Systems

There are several types of livery system, all of which have their pros and cons. Whatever precise system you choose, it will be based on DIY, part-DIY/assisted, full or working.

DIY means it is all down to you, though there should be someone keeping an overall watch to make sure that everything runs smoothly, potential problems are spotted and owners informed. Assisted or part-DIY means that you are responsible for part of the work and the yard owner or staff helps with other tasks.

Full livery means that all your pony's needs are catered for by the yard. Working livery is operated by some riding schools and means that the fee you pay for the pony's keep and care is less than would be the case for full livery, but this is offset by the school being allowed to use him for a specified number of lessons, where he will be ridden by school clients.

Which option?

DIY grass livery is the cheapest form and means that the pony lives out all year round. The advantage is that this mimics a natural lifestyle but, against that, relatively small paddocks and rich grass can turn today's ponies into equine couch potatoes. Food is constantly available without them having to work to find it and they quickly become overweight and prone to problems such as laminitis, a crippling condition of the feet. The opposite of over-rich grazing is a paddock bare of anything other than weeds or ragwort, which should also be avoided in the interest of your pony's health. However, this should not be confused with small, properly managed areas of very short grass used to control a pony's weight.

Grass livery is only an option if the land is well managed, the fencing is safe, shelter is available all year round and a suitable worming programme is in place for all the field occupants. There is more information later on in this chapter on assessing whether or not an environment is safe. If you decide to keep a pony at grass livery, you must be sure that a stable will be made available should he be injured or become ill.

DIY livery which allows the occupants to be turned out all day and stabled at night works well for many owners. It certainly makes it easier to keep a check on your pony's weight.

TIP

Whatever management system you intend to use, you need a back-up system in case the main pony carer is unavailable, perhaps because of illness—though a good livery yard should be able to help in an emergency. As already noted, it makes sense for someone else in the family to learn basic skills such as catching, leading and tying up a pony, though parents usually acquire these skills as a matter of course. Hopefully, you will also be able to build a mutual support network with other pony owners at your yard.

Most yards have farriers who visit regularly and will take on an extra client. You should also find that a yard has contact with one or more local equine vets.

Assisted/part-DIY livery may make life easier for many families and gives you the security of knowing that if you have an emergency, your pony will get his routine care. Some yards offer standard arrangements: for instance, they will turn out your pony in the morning and bring him in at night, dealing with any rugs if necessary. This makes it easier for your pony to have a routine, which will help keep him relaxed. It also makes it easier for the yard to maintain a routine, which adds to its efficiency and means that you do not get a pony who is unhappy because all his friends have either gone out in the field or have come in from it and he is left waiting for his owners.

Full livery is an option usually chosen only by adult owners who do not have time to look after their horses because of work or other commitments. It is rarely appropriate for ponies and for obvious reasons, is the most expensive way of keeping a horse.

Working livery tends to have more disadvantages than advantages. The plus points are that it offers a cheaper way to keep your pony and ensures that he gets enough exercise. Unfortunately, you may find that the yard owner will want to use him at times which conflict with those when you want to ride.

Many people who start off with this system find that they end up feeling that they do not have enough control over who is riding their pony. If it is the only option you can afford, perhaps think about sharing a pony rather than buying one.

Finding the Right Yard

The best way to find a yard where you and your pony will be happy—and it is essential that it suits both of you—is often by word of mouth. If you have been riding at a local school and are offered the chance to keep a pony there, it may seem ideal. Some schools manage to keep school and livery clients happy, but others have to give priority to school clients. This may mean that facilities are not available when you need them: for instance, at weekends.

Also, a location that may be ideal for a riding school is not always ideal for a private owner. If the school is surrounded by busy roads and does not have access to off-road riding, you will miss out on being able to ride in the open, one of the pleasures of owning a pony. Both of you are likely to become bored if you can only ride in an arena and you will not be able to develop your skills as an all-round rider, which is important. Even if you dream of becoming a top showjumper or dressage rider, you need all-round experience first!

Word of mouth is always a good recommendation. If your local riding school does not take liveries, your instructor should know of yards that would be suitable. As always, your Pony Club Branch will be a good source of information and other members may know of vacancies available on their yards.

You will want to feel that you and your pony are part of a friendly, well-run set-up, so when you draw up a shortlist of possible yards, make sure they cater for ponies and young riders and are not specialist competition yards which take only adult clients. Many yards, large and small, now have their own websites, which will enable you to check facilities and prices.

Assessing a yard

It is counterproductive to turn up at a yard and expect to be a given a guided tour, as if staff are busy looking after their charges and facilities they will only ask you to make an appointment. Save time and make the right impression by doing that in the first place.

If you are not confident enough to decide whether a yard and fields are safe and suitable, take someone experienced with you. From a safety point of view, is the yard reasonably neat and tidy or are there mucking-out tools lying around

Ragwort in **(above)** rosette and **(right)** flowering stages.

waiting to trip up the unwary? Are fire extinguishers and emergency telephone numbers in clear sight? The yard does not need to be a blinding vision of white paint and hanging flower baskets, but is it in good repair generally?

Most yard owners will ask you to visit at a quiet time so they can give you their attention. Even so, you should be able to gauge whether there is a calm, friendly atmosphere. If staff are grumpy, the yard is strewn with bedding even though no one is mucking out and stable doors are tied up with baler twine, give it a miss.

Make sure you inspect the fields. Depending on the time of year and weather conditions, they may be muddy in places, especially round gateways, but you do not want to see horses and ponies standing in a sea of mud with not a blade of grass anywhere in sight. Your general impression should be that they are well maintained and not overstocked and that their occupants are in good condition, without being obese or too thin.

Fences and gates should be safe and suitable and in good condition. Barbed wire is not acceptable fencing, as it can cause horrific injuries if a horse runs into or becomes tangled in it. There are many kinds of fencing that are safe for horses, including post and rail and electric fencing. However, fencing of any type will only work if it is properly installed and maintained.

Hedging that is thick enough to form a safe barrier and provide shelter is often cited as the ideal, but takes a long time to become established and many yards do not have people with the time and skill to maintain it. You are more likely to see hedging that has been reinforced with post and rail or electric fencing.

There should be no signs of ragwort, which is poisonous and often fatal to equines. In the rosette stage of growth, it lies flat to the ground and is harder to spot than when it bears its distinctive yellow flowers.

Questions and answers

You will probably find that the yard owner or manager will ask you as many, if not more, questions than you have prepared yourself. This is a good sign, because a yard can only run well if everyone understands his or her responsibilities. Do not be worried about confessing a lack of experience—it is far better than trying to give a false impression that anyone knowledgeable will see through.

There may seem to be a lot of rules. Again, this is a good sign, because it shows that all involved know where they stand. For instance, you should find that the yard owner will insist that you have third party liability insurance and will want your permission to call out a vet if your pony is ill or injured and you cannot be contacted. It might sound frighteningly formal when owning a pony is meant to be a pleasure, but rules like this are essential for everyone, human and equine.

If your overall impressions are good, other things you need to find out include:

- Does someone live on site? This is essential in case of an emergency and for security reasons.
- If you are arranging part livery, what does it comprise? Some yards charge a basic rate and price every task separately, from bringing in and turning out your pony to holding him for the farrier.
- What is the yard's worming policy? Many insist that all animals are wormed according to a set programme, while others leave it up to individual owners. The latter system may work if every owner has a sensible regime, but not if some are less conscientious or, worst of all, don't worm at all.
- Is there enough grazing for your pony to go out in the field every day? Limited turnout causes problems.
- If you are discussing DIY livery, what tasks are you required to do? This may include rota jobs such as picking up droppings from the field and sweeping the yard.
- If your pony is to be stabled part of the time, can you buy bedding and forage through the yard or do you have to buy independently? A large yard which buys in bulk should be able to negotiate better prices.
- Can you arrange for someone to look after your pony if you go on holiday or have an emergency?
- Is the use of facilities such as an outdoor arena included in the price, or is there an extra charge?
- What are the yard's opening and closing hours? Some may not wish owners to be there before or after certain times unless there is a specific reason.
- Are there other young riders based on the yard? You will have more fun if there are people in your age group as well as adults to talk to and ride with.

Make a reservation

When you find a yard you feel happy with, you will probably have to pay a retainer fee if there is already a vacancy. Popular yards may operate a waiting list system, but if there is no guarantee of when a space will become available, you will have to decide whether to keep looking or put your plans on hold until it does.

Only you can decide which is the best option but, if in doubt, wait. Similarly, do not risk keeping a pony at a yard if you feel its standards are not high enough. It is better to wait than to risk his—or your—welfare and safety.

Time preparing to become a pony owner is never wasted. Try to ride as many different types of pony as possible, as long as they are within your capability. Learn as much as you can about horses and ponies in general, because the more you know about how and why they react to things, the better.

Take every opportunity to learn about feeding, shoeing and veterinary care and general management. Offer to groom, clean tack and muck out for friends; riding schools have to be so careful because of insurance and Health and Safety legislation that they may not be able to give you such opportunities on an informal basis, but may let you watch and ask questions. The more skills and knowledge you acquire now, the more confident you will be when you have a pony of your own.

Offering to muck out for a friend will give you experience and help you appreciate the work involved in looking after a pony.

3. Your Perfect Pony

Take Your Partner

While there is no such thing as a perfect pony, you should be able to find a pony who is perfect for you as an owner and rider. To find the right partner, you have to be honest and realistic and appreciate that you are looking for a pony to suit you at the current stage of your riding ability.

There is nothing wrong with being ambitious, but do not think too far ahead. If you are buying your first pony, you should not be tempted by one who has lots of ability as a competition animal but also needs an experienced rider. Nor should you buy a four-year-old who has just been backed, because however honest and well-behaved he is, he will only have started his education and will need someone who can continue it and has the confidence and competence to introduce him to new experiences.

Parents should be particularly wary about buying a pony who is too big for a child, in the hope that the rider will 'grow into him'. It is rather like expecting a small child to ride a bigger brother's or sister's bicycle—the rider will be physically unable to direct and control the pony because of the disparity in their proportions. You cannot apply a leg aid if your leg only comes halfway down the pony's side!

You may have to accept that the pony who is right for you now will not always be your perfect partner. However, it is better to forge a great relationship, build your skills together and eventually find him a home with a smaller/less experienced partner than to damage your and the pony's confidence because you have taken on more than you are ready to cope with.

While these guidelines apply to all pony and rider partnerships, bear in mind that every rider and every pony is an individual. One rider may be happier with a pony who is calm and needs more encouragement, while another will find him boring and enjoy riding one who always seems raring to go. There is no right or wrong: it is all about making the right match for you.

First, second, third

A first pony is, in many ways, the most important one you will ever buy. Ask top riders about the horses they have ridden throughout their careers and there will be some who are memorable and some they can barely remember—but they will all recall their first ponies and what they learned from them, good and bad.

The main job of a first pony is to instil confidence and he should remain calm under all reasonable circumstances. As his rider will usually have ridden only on lessons at a riding school, he will need to be the sort who answers questions, but forgives mistakes. He will not be the sort who goes up a gear as soon as the rider's legs touch his sides, but nor should he be so switched off that a rider can kick repeatedly without getting a response.

Experienced parents, especially those who ride themselves and/or have older children with ponies, may look for a pony suitable to be ridden on a lead rein by a child who is old enough and balanced enough to be safe in the saddle without being supported but does not have the length of leg or muscular strength to control and direct a pony unaided.

This pony must be kind, unflappable, comfortable and responsive to a handler's voice and body language. Not surprisingly, he may be hard to find and if your ambitions lie in the show ring—which means he must have good conformation and correct movement that makes it easy for a little rider to stay balanced—he will probably be very expensive.

A second pony is the next step up in every way. He will be a bit bigger, a little more reactive—if his rider is ready for that—and be able to do a little more. While a first pony may be asked to go over a pole on the ground or a tiny cross-pole fence, either on or off the lead rein as appropriate, a second pony should be one who can be ridden by a child alone, but under supervision.

He should be easy to control in all gaits and capable of jumping a very small course, provided that his rider is also capable of doing this. He should

It is important that a pony suits his rider in terms of height, ability and temperament.

also be suitable for a child to ride in open spaces and, if he is kept in suitable surroundings, to go on escorted hacks.

Once you get to the third pony, you may be looking for one with whom his rider can enjoy more advanced instruction and competing. In general, the ideal partner is one who has good all-round experience, adequate ability and has not been made sour by bad experiences. A pony who has been asked to do more than he is capable of or ready for, especially when jumping, may misbehave or refuse to co-operate. It is not his fault, but it will dishearten most riders.

If you have plenty of experience and can afford him, a competition schoolmaster can teach a rider an awful lot. Be aware, though, that a pony who is super successful with one rider will not automatically be a winner with another. It takes time to build a partnership and a well-schooled pony will not necessarily be an easy ride, purely because he will have been taught to respond quickly to precise instructions.

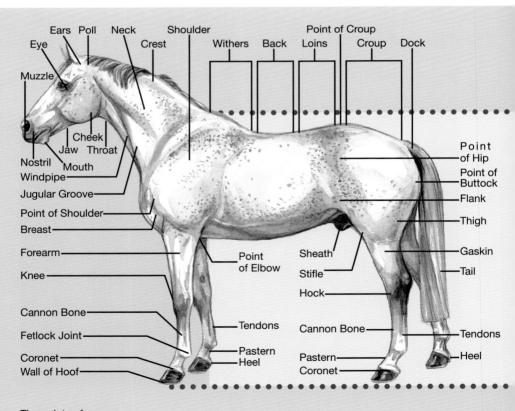

The points of a pony.

Practical Parts

Size, age and gender

It often helps to work out a blueprint for your perfect pony, starting with the basics of height, type, age and gender. If you have been having lessons, your instructor is a good person to ask. In some cases, your age may be a factor, as competition rules sometimes specify that ponies up to a certain height can only be ridden by riders of a certain age. However, in most cases, this will be less important than simple considerations such as whether you will be comfortable riding a particular height and type of pony.

Height is always measured at the highest point of the withers and may be described in hands and inches or centimetres. A hand is four inches, so a 13.2hh pony will be 54ins, or 138cms. The chart below will help you work out what's what. (Mathematicians will notice that the metric measurements

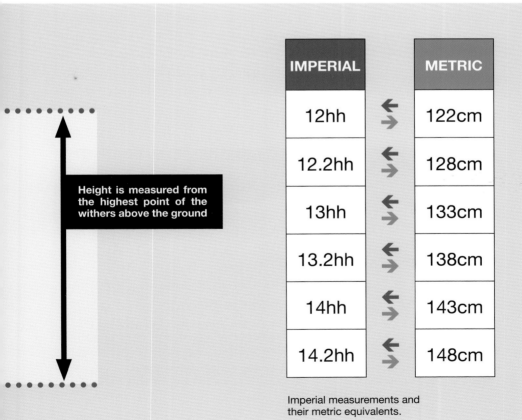

Height is measured from the highest point of the withers above the ground

IMPERIAL		METRIC
12hh	⇄	122cm
12.2hh	⇄	128cm
13hh	⇄	133cm
13.2hh	⇄	138cm
14hh	⇄	143cm
14.2hh	⇄	148cm

Imperial measurements and their metric equivalents.

are actually slightly bigger than their imperial equivalents, but these are the ones which have been adopted by breed societies and competition bodies.)

One thing you will find as you ride different ponies is that while height is an important consideration, a pony's type or breed affects the way he goes and how he feels when you are riding. For instance, a 13.2hh pony who has a long stride and a reasonably long neck will feel bigger to ride than a 14.2hh pony with a short stride and short neck. This is what people mean when they say a horse or pony 'rides big' or 'rides small'.

It is important that a rider feels comfortable, so a first pony, in particular, should not be too wide. A small rider who is halfway to doing the splits will not feel secure, and lack of security equals lack of confidence.

The age of a pony may not be as relevant as his experience and temperament—though, as explained previously, he must have been educated to a standard that matches his rider's experience. Never underestimate an older pony who is in good health, as many work happily and compete, sometimes at top level, into their late teens and beyond.

Does it matter whether you buy a gelding or a mare? That is a question to ask when you have plenty of time for discussion and are ready to hear many different opinions! Undoubtedly, there are many lovely mares and some riders have a particular affinity with them. In general, though, geldings are regarded as easier to deal with because, as castrated males, they are not affected by reproductive urges.

Size, age and gender are important factors to consider when deciding what sort of horse or pony to buy.

Never buy a mare with the idea that you can breed from her later on, unless she is an exceptional animal with a proven record and recorded pedigree, and you have plenty of experience and a healthy bank balance and can, as far as possible, guarantee the future of her offspring. Breeding any foal is a costly business and no matter how fond you may be of a mare, she must have good conformation, temperament, movement and ability to be worth putting in foal.

It is not just a case of money. Even if you intend to keep a foal, your circumstances might change—and trying to find a home for an average or, if you are unlucky, below average pony in a crowded marketplace will be difficult.

Novice owners—and also most experienced ones—should never buy stallions. Although a stallion who has been properly handled and educated may have just as good a temperament as a gelding, the fact that he will retain all his breeding instincts means he needs an owner with specialist knowledge and appropriate facilities. This applies even if a stallion is not used for breeding purposes.

Doubling up

Are you looking for a pony who will be ridden by more than one person? Circumstances or finances mean that some families will need a pony who can be shared, or you may need one who can sometimes be ridden by a parent or other lightweight adult.

While first consideration must be given to the main rider and you do not want to fall into the trap of buying a pony who is too big for a child, a relatively small pony of appropriate build will take a lightweight adult. The large native breeds—those indigenous to the British Isles—will carry most adults, within reason.

The same applies to small cobs. With the exception of the Welsh Section D, also called the Welsh Cob, a cob is not a breed—though he may have recorded breeding. He is a type, characterised by his solid build. You will find more information about breeds and types later in this chapter.

The colour question

Most people have preferences regarding coat colour, but there are so many other considerations to take into account that it should be bottom of the list of physical characteristics. Of course, it is lovely to imagine galloping along the beach on a beautiful palomino, his golden coat gleaming in the sun and his white mane and tail streaming in the wind—but you would have just as much fun if he was bay, brown or chestnut.

Everyone has different tastes. Some people find greys particularly attractive while others think of them in terms of the hard work needed to keep them clean. Also, attitudes and fashions change. At one time, skewbalds and piebalds, with their mixture of white and dark patches, were frowned upon; now, they are incredibly popular.

Although some colours are supposed be associated with particular characteristics, there is no evidence to support this. In particular, there is no more reason to support the theory that chestnuts are more likely to be hot-headed than there is for supposing that red-haired people have fiery tempers.

There is an old saying—one of many—that a good horse is never a bad colour. There are two ways you can interpret this, but the sensible way is that if you like a pony, it does not matter what colour he is.

Temperament

There is an old saying that the most important part of a horse or pony is the bit between his ears: in other words, his brain! Certainly a good temperament, which is another word for character, is essential, but defining it is not always as easy as it seems and you have to decide what it means for your particular needs and circumstances—with one proviso.

When top riders talk about a horse having the right temperament, they mean that he should accept and cope well with the work he has to do for his particular job. They often talk about a 'trainable' temperament rather than a 'good' temperament. Such riders might not be concerned if a horse is grumpy in the stable, or even if he needs careful handling because of a tendency to kick or bite.

However, all ponies who are going to be handled and ridden by children and young riders must have good manners and show no signs of aggression. (It has to be said that the same applies to most horses intended for non-professional owners!) No matter how wonderful a pony is to ride, you cannot risk a child's safety. Nor can you expect a young owner to enjoy spending time with a pony who is difficult to handle.

A pony should be amenable with his own kind as well as with riders and handlers. Riding in company, whether out hacking or at a Pony Club rally, is an essential part of owning a pony and you do not want to have to worry that a pony will kick out at any others who come near him.

Assuming that the pony will be hacked out, it is essential that he is good in traffic. There are some things you can compromise on, but this is not one of them: it is literally a matter of life and death. There is no such thing as a bombproof pony, but you cannot risk one who is unreliable on the roads. Even if you will be keeping him in quiet surroundings, you cannot guarantee that you will not meet a delivery lorry, a car driver in too much of a hurry, or a tractor.

From a parent's point of view, it is a real bonus if a pony is good to catch, shoe, load and travel. They may be problems that you can overcome, but life is a lot easier if you do not have to.

Temperament and power

When you learn to drive, you do not go straight out and buy a Ferrari, even if you can afford it, as too much horsepower in the hands of a novice is potentially dangerous. The same applies to real life horsepower and with a pony, you are talking not only about different levels of power and reactions, but the fact that he has a mind of his own.

Even though a pony may have an essentially good temperament in that he is polite to handle and complies with correctly given aids, one who is sensitive to the subtlest leg or rein aid, or to a small shift in the rider's weight, may be too

A pony must be suitable for a child to handle as well as to ride, though children should always have the supervision of a knowledgeable adult.

much for a novice rider. To start with, at least, it is better to feel that a pony is a little lacking in power rather than having more than you can cope with.

In particular, a pony for an inexperienced or nervous rider should be calm and laid-back about most things. Were he a person, he would take everything in his stride and perhaps even be a bit lazy.

If you are more experienced and confident, you might find a pony with this sort of attitude boring or frustrating to ride, because he will not have enough natural 'oomph'. Having said that, some ponies can seem lazy because they are not schooled and/or kept in the right way. A fat pony who looks like a blob on four legs will behave accordingly and one who has switched off mentally because his rider is always kicking him will not respond to light aids.

A competent rider who has a balanced, independent seat and more all-round experience than someone looking for a first pony will usually enjoy riding a pony who is responsive to the aids and generally quicker to react. There is a difference between a pony who is responsive and one who may be described as 'sensitive' or 'sharp'. The latter will only suit a rider who is established, competent, confident and sensitive enough to know how much to ask.

Stereotypical behaviour

As you start looking for a pony, you may come across animals who exhibit stereotypical behaviour. This is repetitive behaviour which used to be called 'stable vices' and is still referred to as such by some people. This is really an unfair term, as it is now generally agreed that the behaviour is an attempt to reduce stress caused by confinement in a stable.

TIP

There is nothing wrong with being a cautious rider. In fact, every rider should retain a degree of caution, because otherwise, you risk being foolhardy and may put yourself and your pony at risk. Lack of experience or confidence does not mean that you are a coward! In any case, your confidence will grow as you gain experience.

However, if you are really frightened of something, perhaps of cantering in company or jumping, talk to your instructor about it. This way, you will be able to find strategies to build your confidence and overcome your fear. Remember that it takes more courage to admit that you are nervous about something than to be a rider who takes risks without thinking about possible consequences.

There is nothing wrong with stabling a pony for short periods and there are times when it may be necessary or even simply convenient to do so. However, remember that by nature, horses and ponies need to spend most of their time in a suitable outdoors environment.

There are three main forms of stereotypical behaviour: weaving, crib-biting and wind-sucking. The last two sometimes, though not always, go together. All may be exhibited in different degrees, from mild to severe.

A mild weaver moves his head from side to side over the stable door. In severe cases, he may sway through his whole body and shift his weight from one foot to the other. A crib-biter fixes his teeth on a handy surface, such as a stable door or fence rail. Wind-sucking, where the horse or pony gulps in air, may accompany crib-biting but is occasionally seen alone.

It is now generally accepted that stereotypical behaviour stimulates the production of endorphins, natural 'feel-good' chemicals that reduce stress levels. However, if the behaviour is marked, it may have health implications. For instance, pronounced weaving may put strain on a horse's limbs and a wind-sucker may be prone to colic (abdominal pain, classed as a veterinary emergency).

The easiest way to minimise or prevent such behaviours is to keep the pony out 24/7, thus reducing stress. It is extremely rare to see a horse or pony weaving in the open, though unfortunately, some crib-biters will carry out the behaviour using a fence or similar surface.

The behaviours described are accepted as being the most problematical and must be declared if a horse or pony is offered for sale by auction. Another stereotypical behaviour, box-walking, can be just as much a problem but is not declarable under auction conditions. Box-walkers, as the name suggests, walk round and round their stables, which not only imposes physical strain but means they may be difficult to keep weight on. They also churn up their bedding, leading to a dirty stable that needs topping up with clean bedding more frequently.

Attitudes towards stereotypical behaviour vary, but unless the pony is a superstar, it will reduce his value. It may also make him less welcome at some livery yards. There is still a commonly held belief that other horses and ponies will copy the unwanted behaviour, though research shows this is not the case. However, on a more practical level, crib-biters can cause expensive damage to buildings and fences.

Whether or not you are prepared to accept such behaviour is purely a matter of personal choice. Sometimes, a horse or pony may exhibit it for a short period when he moves to a new home and feels insecure, but will stop when he settles in.

Breeds and Types

When you start looking for a pony, you will find some who have recorded breeding and some who have no known pedigree. Also, some will be purebred examples of native ponies—those indigenous to the British Isles—and others will be of mixed breeding. It is often possible to guess a pony's origins just from his looks.

Does it matter if you know how a pony is bred? There is no single answer to that. If you want a pony to compete in showing classes for registered breeds, then obviously it does, but if you are looking for an all-round friend, it probably will not matter. A 'Heinz 57' can be just as much fun and give just as much pleasure as one with a pedigree, so it is really a matter of choice.

It may also affect your budget. A purebred, registered pony—particularly one of the large breeds, which can be ridden by adults of average size and weight—will usually be more expensive than his equivalent of unknown breeding.

It is useful to know the characteristics of Britain's nine native breeds. All have their devotees and all can be trained to go correctly, though some are naturally more athletic under saddle than others. However, sympathetic patience and schooling can achieve wonders and many of the heavier breeds,

Connemara ponies can be suitable for children and adults.

New Forest ponies in their natural habitat.

Dartmoor ponies are willing and athletic.

Highland ponies are versatile and up to weight.

such as Highland ponies, compete successfully in dressage and enjoy jumping.

There are two horse breeds which are also particularly important; the Arabian and the Thoroughbred. Both have been introduced into Britain's pony breeds at some stage, often to add refinement. In general terms, the more Thoroughbred blood a pony possesses, the more sensitive and less hardy he is likely to be. For example, a pony who is three-quarters Thoroughbred will not grow a coat as thick as that of a native pony and will need more food to maintain his weight in winter than a native doing similar work.

The breed societies responsible for promoting and registering native ponies set height limits to preserve their characteristics. You may find ponies, especially Connemaras, who have grown over these limits. This will preclude them from competing in breed society showing classes, but has no effect on their general all-round ability.

A brief description of the native pony breeds follows.

THE CONNEMARA is arguably the most popular native breed and is attractive, versatile and athletic. Officially, heights range from about 12.2hh (128cm) to 14.2hh (148cm).

THE DALES pony is a real weight-carrier. He is strong, hardy and, although solidly built, can be light on his feet, with a particularly powerful trot. Height is usually between 14hh (143cm) and 14.2hh (148cm) but the Dales Pony Society does not specify an upper height limit.

THE DARTMOOR pony often makes a great riding pony for smaller children, as his smooth movement makes him comfortable and he is not too wide. He has a maximum height of 12.2hh (128cm).

THE EXMOOR is the oldest of the British pony breeds and is incredibly strong for his maximum size of 12.3hh (130cm). Although many Exmoors make good riding ponies, this breed tends not to be as naturally athletic as some of the others.

Exmoor ponies can carry more weight than their small size suggests.

Shetland ponies are often used to give children their first introduction to riding.

Fell and Dale ponies are comfortable, active rides.

THE FELL pony has many characteristics in common with the Dales, such as coat colour—predominantly black, dark brown, bay and, less commonly, grey. The breed height limit is 14hh (143cm).

HIGHLAND PONIES were bred to carry heavy deer carcasses and are up to most riders' weights. Their maximum height is 14.2hh (148cm).

THE NEW FOREST has a height range from around 12.2hh to 14.2hh (128–148cm). Smaller ponies are narrow enough for small children and ponies who have been bred or turned out on the New Forest are inevitably good in traffic, because they see so much of it.

THE SHETLAND is the smallest of all the native breeds and is measured in inches rather than hands. The size must not exceed 42in (107cm). When trained correctly, the Shetland makes a good first pony, but he must be treated as the proper pony he is and not just as a pet or a lawnmower on four legs!

THE WELSH ponies are represented by four breeds, divided into Sections A, B, C and D. The Section A is also known as the Welsh Mountain pony and the Section B, as the Welsh pony. The Section C is the Welsh pony of cob type and the section D, the Welsh Cob.

Breed society rules say that Section As must not exceed 12.2hh (128cm) and the upper height for Section Bs is 13.2hh (138cm). The Section C is a stockier type of pony, also with a 13.2hh (138cm) height limit. The Welsh Section D has no upper height limit, though most are between 14.2hh (148cm) and 15.2hh (158cm).

Welsh Section A and B ponies can be ridden by children and small adults.

The Welsh Section D is the largest of the Welsh breeds.

Key Thoughts

Many of the subjects covered in later chapters of this book will be relevant to all would-be pony owners, whether they are looking for a first pony, have graduated to a second or are getting serious about competing. However, when you are drawing up your blueprint, you might want to think about the following:

- A first pony might be the most important one you could ever buy. The experiences you share with him, good and bad, will shape your future riding life.
- Good conformation—physical proportions—means a pony will be more likely to stay sound and find his work easier, as explained in Chapter 5. However, one who is technically no oil painting but is a pleasure to handle and ride will be worth his weight in gold. Conversely, a breathtakingly good-looking pony who is difficult to handle and/or ride will be more trouble than he is worth.
- A pony who has been perfect for one member of your family might not be perfect for a younger brother or sister who has a different build or temperament. You might be able to hand down bikes and riding clothes, but you cannot always hand down ponies.
- Parents must remember that, while there is nothing wrong with being ambitious for their children, they should resist any temptation to impose their own ambitions on them. Nor should children feel that they have to share the interests of other members of the family, or live up to their reputations. One child might be a demon cross-country rider and have a shelf full of trophies, while a brother or sister may have more sedate tastes and not want to compete. In this respect there is no such thing as right or wrong—all that matters is that riders enjoy what they do.
- If your child wants to compete, the fact that a pony has been an out-and-out winner with his previous owner, or with an older brother or sister, does not mean he will automatically be the same for a new rider. It takes time to settle into a new job and establish a new working relationship, for ponies as well as people.
- You can choose your pony, but a pony cannot choose his owner. You have a responsibility to him to do all you can to make sure he is the right one for you.

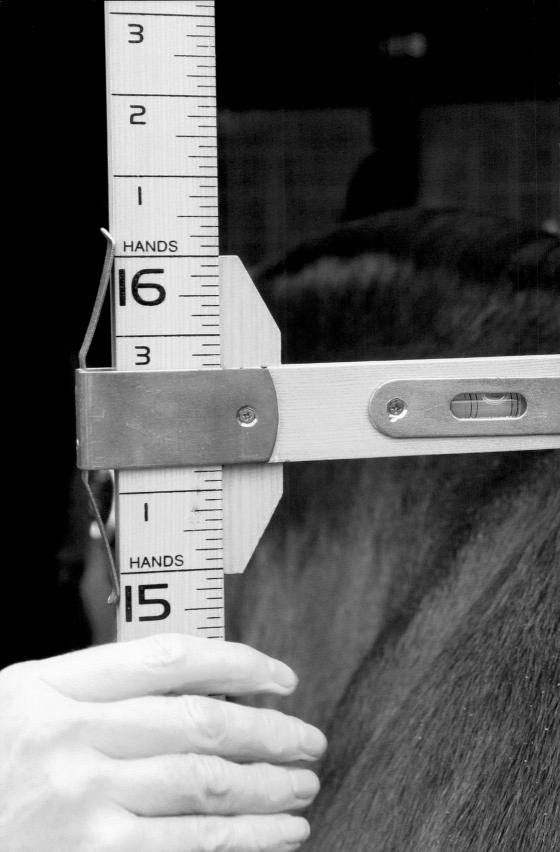

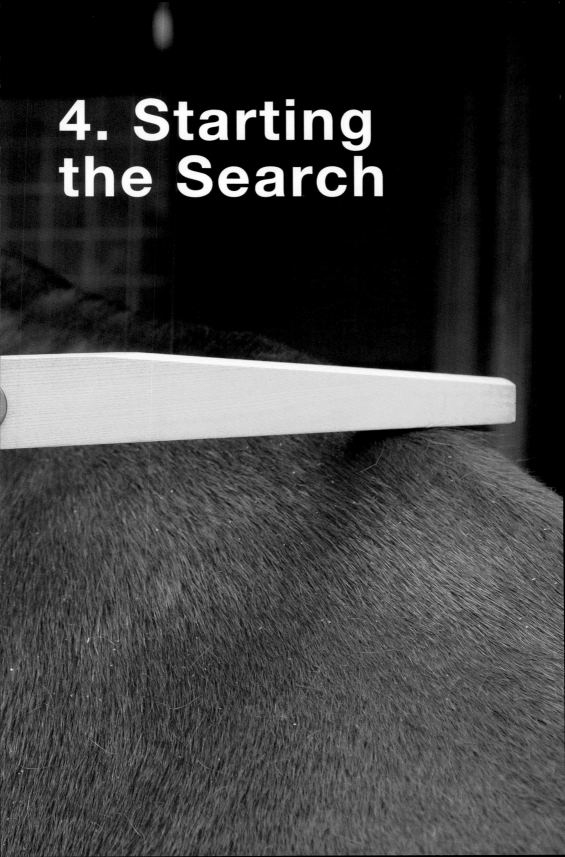

4. Starting the Search

Once you've created a profile of your ideal pony, you can start the exciting—and perhaps frustrating—business of looking at likely sounding prospects.

Why frustrating? Although you might be lucky and find that the first advert you read or the first pony you hear about is the perfect one to fit into your family, it is more likely that you will see some who are unsuitable before hitting the jackpot.

That makes it sound as if buying a pony means taking a gamble. In some ways, you are, because a pony is a living creature with a mind of his own and every rider and pony partnership takes time to gel. You may also find cases where, inadvertently or, unfortunately, deliberately, a seller misrepresents a pony to get a sale.

That is where the Latin phrase *caveat emptor*—buyer beware—is so important. When you are buying an animal, whether a hamster, a puppy or a pony, you can never eliminate all the risks. However, you can minimise them and it is essential to take the time and effort to do so, for the sake of the pony as well as that of the rider and the family bank account.

Never buy a pony without seeing and trying him, no matter how persuasive the seller and no matter how many photographs and videos they are able to send you. There have been many cases of buyers falling for animals on the strength of this and finding that the reality does not match up.

If you do not already know the pony, the fact that it is so easy to send photographs and videos may make you feel that it is not worth going to look at a prospect if the seller is not prepared to do this, especially if you would have to travel a long distance.

Laying Down the Law

Although it may sound depressing, you need to be aware of consumer law. We live in a litigation-conscious society and there are many cases of buyers suing sellers because they believe they have been sold horses or ponies who are unsound or unsuitable. This is distressing and potentially expensive for both parties and in many cases, can be avoided. Hopefully, this book will help you walk safely through the minefield.

Opposite: A horse or pony described as a showjumper must be capable of jumping a course of fences.

All purchases, whether you are talking about a pony or a washing machine, are governed by the Sales of Goods Act 1979. In simple terms, this means that whatever you buy must be of reasonable quality and be fit for purpose. In terms of buying a pony, being of reasonable quality could mean, for instance, that the pony is not lame. Being fit for purpose means that a pony bought for a particular job, such as showjumping, is capable of doing it. Common sense must apply and inevitably, things may not be as simple as they sound.

So far, so good. However, you only get the full protection of the Sale of Goods Act if you buy from a dealer: someone who buys and sells on a commercial basis. If you buy from a private seller, your protection is limited unless you can prove that the seller knew, or ought to have known, that the pony was unsuitable or unfit for purpose.

In either case, doing everything you can to avoid problems is much better than trying to deal with them after the event.

Ways to Buy

There are three ways to buy a pony: from a private seller, from a dealer and from an auction. All have their pros and cons, though buying from an auction is not something novice buyers should consider. Information about the auction process is included here for information and as a warning.

All sellers should be honest about whether they are private or otherwise. It's a tricky definition, but anyone who has a pony for sale every two or three months would probably not be regarded as a private seller.

Reputable dealers rely on their reputation to make a living and trade openly. The people to watch out for are the ones who claim to be private sellers, but are selling a pony purely to try to make a profit. In some cases, they may be unaware that they are trading commercially, but that does not alter the fact that they are doing so.

Private sales

Most ponies will be sold privately, usually because they have been outgrown or, sadly, because their riders have lost interest. The advantage of buying privately is that if the sale is for genuine reasons, the seller will be anxious to find the pony a good, suitable home and will be honest about everything, from what he has done to any problems that have been encountered.

The disadvantage is that some sellers might not be knowledgeable enough to recognise whether or not a pony would be suitable for your purpose. You might also be unlucky enough to meet a seller who has bought the wrong pony and, being anxious to offload a problem, is economical with the truth. However, sensible buyers who get the right advice should be able to spot potential problems.

Another disadvantage of buying privately is that a private seller may find it difficult to set a realistic price and ask an inflated sum.

Dealers

Forget the stereotypical image of a dealer as a trickster who will misrepresent everything from age to soundness to get a sale. There are some dishonest dealers, just as there are dishonest private sellers, but the majority of professional traders are honest.

Few dealers sell first and second ponies, though there are some who specialise in competition ponies. An established competition pony with a good record will not be cheap. Nor will a potential top-class animal, in any sphere—and remember that 'potential' only translates to 'actual' with the right rider who has the back-up of a good trainer. Most ponies with potential will be young animals, so the same provisos apply.

If you pick the right person, there are advantages of buying from a dealer. The most obvious is that you get the full protection of the Sale of Goods Act. You will also be buying from someone who knows how to assess ponies and—just as important—potential buyers. It is not in a dealer's interest to sell you a pony who is unsuitable, as your results will act as an advert—good or bad—for him or her.

A good dealer is a good sales person and as such will know how to present a pony in the best light. Dealers also know the state of the market and while you will probably not find a bargain at a dealer's, you should find an animal who is described and priced realistically. In the long run, it may be better to pay more for the right competition pony from a dealer than to buy a cheaper one from a less knowledgeable private seller.

Note that cheaper does not mean cheap—a good performance pony will always find a good price and while a professional seller should be realistic about setting a figure, a private one may not be. That is, of course, a generalisation.

Dealers and agents

Most dealers source their stock from regular suppliers within the horse buying trade. They may also take in horses and ponies in part exchange, assess them and perhaps improve their way of going and then sell them.

As far as your legal rights go, it is important to know whether the dealer owns a pony or is selling on behalf of the owner. In the latter scenario, the dealer is acting as an agent rather than as a vendor and if you buy a pony sold this way and have problems, you would need to take redress against the owner and the dealer. This all sounds very depressing and, hopefully, your research and the precautions you take will help you avoid problems. However, it is better to be aware of such issues than to go in blindly.

Auctions

There are many types of auction, from small sales to high-powered specialist auctions. At the latter, racehorses or potential international competition horses may change hands for big money. Smaller sales include those organised by breed societies or other bodies.

For experienced owners and riders, buying at auction is accepted practice. However, it is not a suitable avenue for the less experienced to take. Sadly, there are still some small sales that become a dumping ground for animals with behavioural or physical problems and the auction process does not give the opportunity to assess a child's pony in enough depth.

By all means go to one of the specialist sales and enjoy an exciting and educational day out, but do not go to your local market and expect to find your perfect pony there. You may be lucky, but the chances of buying a problem on four legs are so high that it's really not worth the risk.

A pony may be freeze-marked for security.

On the Trail

There are many ways to find likely sounding prospects and it is worth exploring all of them. One of the best, especially for first and second ponies, is the local horse and pony network, starting with Pony Club Branches. Tell Branch officials and instructors what you are looking for and the chances are that you will not only hear of ponies for sale and loan, but will also get potted histories to go with them. Be totally honest about the rider's ability and experience, as that way, you will not waste your time, or anyone else's.

The Pony Club's own website has a special classified advertisements section where you will find ponies of all types offered for sale. Many Branches also have their own websites and again, these may include adverts.

Use all forms of networking, from phone calls to social websites. Sites such as Facebook have many pages and groups set up to allow members to advertise horses, ponies and everything equestrian. As always, adult supervision is essential if children are allowed to look at such sites.

In addition to websites, you will find adverts detailing ponies for sale everywhere from notice boards in local saddlers to equestrian magazines. As mentioned earlier, on websites some sellers now post videos of their ponies in action, which, even when carefully edited, give an idea of whether the reality matches up to the description. If a pony described as well-schooled is shown carting a child round a field, it is safe to assume that there has been some poetic licence.

It's a bonus if a pony is good to clip.

You need to decide at the start how far you are prepared to travel to look at suitable-sounding prospects, as both time and fuel are expensive. Some buyers will literally travel to the other end of the country to see what sounds like the perfect pony, while others set a mileage limit. In most cases, you should be able to find a pony in your region, though buyers of serious competition animals may feel that distance is no object.

Translating the adverts

If you want to sell something, you describe it in favourable terms. This applies to ponies, so expect to look at a magazine or website and find ponies described in such glowing terms that you expect to see them wearing haloes. This means that you need to read not only the adverts, but the bits between the lines.

Fortunately, most people now include at least a photograph of their pony. Even if it is not particularly good, a knowledgeable person will be able to tell if terms such as 'stunning' and 'excellent conformation' are realistic or optimistic.

Look for what is stated and what is glossed over or omitted. 'Hacks out safely in all traffic alone and in company' is clear. 'Hacks out' means very little, because the pony could be a nightmare while doing so. 'Hacks out in light traffic' may mean that this is all the current owners meet, but could also mean

ABBREVIATIONS

AA	Anglo-Arab	**NF**	New Forest
BD	British Dressage	**NPS**	National Pony Society
BE	British Eventing	**ODE**	one-day event
BS	British Showjumping	**PC**	Pony Club
BSPA	British Skewbald and Piebald Association	**RIHS**	Royal International Horse Show
BSPS	British Show Pony Society	**SHP**	show hunter pony
CHAPS	Coloured Horse and Pony Society	**SJ**	show-jump
		TB	Thoroughbred
FR	first ridden	**TBx**	Thoroughbred crossed with another breed, or a pony who has one **TB** parent and another of unknown breeding.
HOYS	Horse of the Year Show		
HT	hunter trials		
LD	long distance		
LR	lead rein	**WHP**	working hunter pony
M & M	mountain and moorland	**XC**	cross-country

that the pony throws a wobbly if he meets any vehicle larger than a car.

As you read adverts, you will find recurring initials and phrases. Some of the commonest and their meanings are given below, but be aware that some terms are often used indiscriminately. For instance, an experienced competition pony may be described as a schoolmaster when he is actually a difficult ride. Also, some adverts may be phrased particularly carefully. 'Has evented' may mean that the pony has been successful in this discipline, but may also mean that he bolted in the dressage phase and refused at the first fence.

COMMON PHRASES

Affiliated winnings	A pony who has won prize money in competitions organised by British Dressage, British Eventing or British Showjumping.
Always placed	While this literally means that the pony has been awarded a prize of some sort at every competition in which he has taken part, this phrase is often used to describe one who is successful on a regular basis. The questions to ask are, of course, how regularly he has competed and at what level.
Backed and ridden away	A pony at the start of his education who has been ridden, but not schooled.
Bombproof	Often used to describe a pony who is quiet in all respects. There is, of course, no such thing.
Clean-limbed	Has no blemishes.
Confidence giver	A well-behaved, obedient pony who will help build a rider's confidence.
Easy to do	Well-mannered and good to look after.
Forward-going	Ideally, responsive and not lazy…or a euphemism for a pony who pulls or rushes.
Good to BCST	Good to box, clip, shoe and in traffic.
Green	Inexperienced and needs educating.
Schoolmaster/ mistress	An experienced pony who, if given the correct aids, will give the correct response.

Questions to ask

Ask plenty of questions before arranging to see a pony. This will save you wasted time and transport costs and a genuine seller will appreciate that time spent on the telephone is not wasted. If you find yourself answering as many questions as you ask, it is usually a good sign and means that the seller is trying to ensure a good match.

Do not waste your own or a seller's time by enquiring about ponies who are much more expensive than you can afford. While many people will be prepared to negotiate a price to a good home, or lower a price if they do not sell at their original figure, it is unlikely that anyone would sell you a £5,000 pony for £1,500.

Here are some specific points to consider:

- Ask whether the pony has a passport. It is illegal for anyone to sell a horse or pony without one. You should perhaps become suspicious if told 'Yes, but it's not available at present.'
- Double-check the pony's height. Has the seller measured him, or is it a guess? Some guesses are more accurate than others and it is a waste of time going to see a 13.2hh (138cm) pony who turns out to be nearer 12.2hh (128cm). Anyone buying a pony to show or compete seriously will need to make sure he has a relevant height certificate from the Joint Measurement Board—which acts on behalf of breed societies and competition organisations—or will measure into an appropriate category.
- Be equally careful about age. Can it be verified by breed papers or is the owner relying on dentition or hearsay? Most people still rely on dentition as a good guide to ageing, but it is not always accurate and the older the pony, the more difficult it is to tell his age by looking at his teeth. Although precise age might not be a major criterion, it is essential to have a reasonable

TIP

Use the power of the internet to your advantage. Type a seller's telephone number into a search engine such as Google and see if it is linked to other adverts. This is not only a good way of verifying whether a private seller is just that, or someone who sells so regularly that he or she would be more accurately described as a dealer. You may also find the same pony advertised on different websites at different prices—if he was not sold at one price, a seller may advertise him elsewhere more cheaply, but leave the original advert in case it attracts a buyer.

guideline. For instance, while it might not matter that a good first pony is 15, you would not want to buy a 15-year-old presented as a 9-year-old.

- Ask how long the seller has owned him. This applies more to private sellers; you would have to be wary of a private seller wanting to part with a pony bought a couple of months previously, whereas dealers usually need to sell animals quickly to make their necessary profit.

- Ask what sort of job has the pony been doing and with what type of rider. This should help give an idea of whether or not he is suitable for your family. Describe the potential rider's height, weight, age and ability, tell the seller what you need the pony to do and ask if it sounds whether or not he will be suitable. If the answer is 'no', you have at least been lucky enough to talk to someone honest. However, no matter how firmly a seller tells you that the pony will be perfect for you in every way, no one knows until you see and try him.

- Ask how he is kept. Does he live out all the time, or is he out in the day and stabled at night?

- Ask whether he is good in all traffic. Some sellers, particularly dealers, may advertise animals with phrases such as 'good in all traffic met to date' to cover themselves. It is up to you to get a more detailed description of what this means.

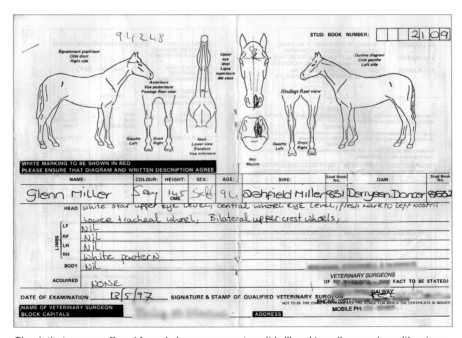

Check that a pony offered for sale has a passport, as it is illegal to sell an equine without one.

- Ask whether he hacks out alone if necessary, or whether he is only reliable hacking out in company. This may or may not be relevant to your situation and you cannot criticise a seller who cannot answer if, for safety reasons, his present rider is only allowed to hack in company.
- Ask whether he is good to handle, catch, shoe and clip. All ponies intended for young riders should be polite and friendly to handle. A pony who is difficult to catch will stretch anyone's patience and not every farrier will be prepared to work with one who is difficult to shoe. Ponies who are nervous to clip often come round with patient handling, but it is a minus point.
- Ask whether he shows signs of any stereotypical behaviour—does he weave, crib-bite, wind-suck or box-walk? If the answer is 'no', there is no problem. If it is something along the lines of, 'Only at feed time and only very slightly' or 'He did it the first day he arrived and has never done it since', then the behaviour has been declared and you have no comeback, even if you get him home and find that he weaves for 23 hours out of 24.
- If you intend to travel a pony in a trailer, ask whether this one travels calmly when transported this way, or is he only happy in a horsebox?
- Ask whether he loads easily, or whether he can be difficult.
- Ask whether he is vaccinated against equine influenza and tetanus. A private seller who has not vaccinated a pony will probably not have bothered to worm him or have dental checks carried out, either. These are not always insurmountable problems, though a long-term owner who has never wormed a pony will have made the animal vulnerable to long-term damage. Such basic lack of care should make you wonder about the seller's knowledge, skills or sense of responsibility. Sadly, dealers rarely vaccinate unprotected animals, because it cuts into their profit margin and they know that a conscientious buyer will get it done.
- Ask whether, during his current ownership, he has had any problems requiring veterinary attention.
- Ask if he has been freeze-marked or identity chipped for security purposes.
- Find out what sort of bit he is ridden in. Hopefully, he will go in a simple snaffle for most things, though it is not necessarily a problem if he is ridden in a different bit at times—for instance, when jumping. However, you do not want a first pony who is ridden in a potentially severe bit, as this suggests he can pull or become strong.
- Ask why he is for sale. There are a variety of answers that may be satisfactory, ranging from a rider who has outgrown him to a child losing interest.

- It is always worth making it clear that you know there is no such thing as the perfect pony for every situation and asking if this one has any issues that need managing. For example, you might be told that a pony dominates his field companions or can become strong when cantering at the back of a group. It is then up to you to decide if this would be manageable or not.

Ready to view

When you decide you have found a pony to look at, get clear directions including the full address and postcode. It is amazing how many people give vague directions to a yard and say 'You can't miss it' when the opposite is true.

Fix a date and time and make sure you have telephone numbers for the seller and, if the pony is kept at livery, for the yard. Give the seller your number and ask to be informed if the pony is sold before you get the chance to see him. If you change your mind, perhaps because you find a perfect prospect beforehand, let the seller know.

There is no excuse for looking at ponies you know you cannot afford even after reasonable negotiation, or trying those you have no intention of buying under the excuse of seeing what is on the market.

The word soon gets round and once you are labelled as a joy rider, you will find people are less inclined to be honest and helpful.

It's a good sign if a horse or pony wears a simple snaffle bridle.

5. Conformation and Movement

Shaping Up

Ponies, like people, come in all shapes and sizes, from finely built, elegant show ponies to chunky natives and cob types. Different owners have different preferences and requirements and you cannot say that one type is better than another.

While looks are not the be all and end all of everything, conformation—which means the way a pony is built—is important. Good conformation, where proportions and angles are as near to the ideal as possible, means biomechanical efficiency. A pony with good conformation is theoretically more likely to stay sound than one who, for instance, has badly conformed legs or poor quality feet. There are many other variables to consider, such as workload, but the odds are in his favour.

It is also fair to say that a pony whose proportions are correct will find it easier to work than one who is not so well made. For example, although correct schooling can work wonders, a pony who is higher at the back end than the front will find it harder to work in balance, because he is naturally on his forehand and 'going downhill'.

Similarly, a pony who has straighter than ideal angles to his shoulder and pasterns will tend to have an up and down action rather than a smoother, lower stride and will not be as comfortable to ride.

Learn as much about conformation as you can before buying a pony. Assessing a pony's make and shape comes through practice and experience. When you are riding different ponies, compare what each feels like to what he looks like.

If you go to a show or event where top riders are competing, look at their horses' and ponies' conformation. You will find that in some disciplines, those who do well are not classically beautiful. Their riders know how to get the best out of them and how to make sure they are fit enough to cope with their jobs. There are also superstar riders who make horses and ponies look easy when they are not—and horses and ponies whose temperament and talent, combined with the fact that they have the right rider, allow them to defy the odds.

There is no such thing as a horse or pony with perfect conformation and one of the most fascinating and difficult challenges is not just identifying good and bad points, but deciding what is acceptable and what is not ideal, but should not cause a problem. Whether or not a defect is likely to cause a problem depends on its severity and whether or not it is compounded by other conformation faults.

There is no such thing as a perfect horse or pony, but one with good conformation will find his work easier.

Conformation is also about 'horses for courses'. Those who ride Western-style require their horses to go with a lower head carriage than in other disciplines. A head and neck set on slightly lower than, say, a warmblood dressage horse is a natural conformation trait of the Quarter Horse, a specialist breed for this discipline.

At top class, specialist level, different jobs may alter priorities. A racehorse trainer will not have exactly the same checklist as, say, a rider looking for a potential dressage star. Also, common sense tells you that a first pony who will be asked to work steadily on a lead rein will not be under as much pressure as a second or third pony who is working much harder and at a higher level.

Whatever job your pony is intended for, there are general guidelines. You do not need to be obsessed by conformation, unless you are looking for a show pony, but you do need to keep it in mind. You also have a safety net in that, when you buy a pony, you will hopefully have a pre-purchase examination carried out by a vet (see Chapter 7) so any major problems should be identified and explained to you.

Above: Any horse or pony can be trained for dressage up to a certain level, but experienced riders who want to specialise in the sport have more demanding requirements.

Opposite: The Quarter horse is the classic breed for Western riding.

Weighing it up

It is much easier to assess conformation when a pony is in correct condition, not overweight. Unfortunately, many horses and ponies are too fat and obesity is as great a health risk in animals as it is in people. One of the biggest dangers facing a fat pony is the risk of laminitis, a crippling and painful condition of the feet.

The best way to judge condition is to learn how to score body fat levels. The most up to date method of doing this is by hands-on as well as visual assessment. You may be shown how to do this at a Pony Club rally and information is available through publications and website videos from organisations such as the Blue Cross and World Horse Welfare.

Head versus heart

You might hear people say that they saw a pony looking over a stable door and immediately decided to buy him. Fine—as long as the rest of him matches up! Try to let your head rule your heart, difficult as it may be.

Assessing Conformation

Overall impressions

Start by looking at a pony as a whole, without focusing on any particular part. He should look as if the front end matches the back end and that his limbs match his body. You do not want to see a powerful front end coupled with a weedy back end, or spindly legs under a chunky body. Both these problems will increase the strain on his limbs.

Feet and limbs

Once you have an overall picture, build a detailed view. Start from the ground up by looking at the pony's feet and limbs, because they are the main weight-bearing and concussion-absorbing structures.

Ideally, the feet should be two matching pairs. Hind feet are usually slightly smaller than forefeet, but each pair should be the same size and shape. The size should relate to that of the pony—you do not want to see a chunky 14.2hh (148cm) with Shetland pony type feet, or an elegant show pony with 'soup plates'.

The soles of the feet should be slightly concave, as flat feet are prone to bruising. Check the angle at which the foot joins the limb: there should be a

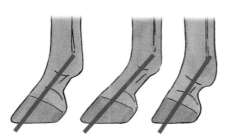

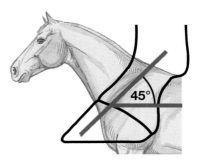

From left to right: A pastern with correct conformation; a weak, sloping pastern; an upright pastern.

The angle of a pony's shoulder usually mirrors the angle of the pastern.

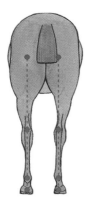

From left to right:
Correct conformation of the hindlegs viewed from the rear and side; cow hocks; sickle hocks.

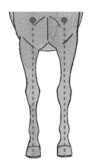

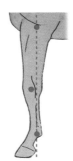

From left to right: Correct conformation of the forelegs viewed from the front and side; a foreleg which is over at the knee; a foreleg which is back at the knee.

continuous slope from the pastern down the hoof. If the angle is broken, the foot and limb will be more susceptible to concussion and strain.

Some people find it difficult to tell the difference between bad conformation and poor farriery. If a pony has not had his feet trimmed at frequent enough intervals, his feet will be too long and his heels too low. Again, a pre-purchase veterinary examination will identify any problems and whether they relate to conformation or to feet which are not trimmed in correct balance.

Poor quality feet which continually crumble or split make it difficult to keep shoes on a pony. Native ponies and those with a high percentage of native blood tend to have better quality feet than some horses. Some breeds, such as Fell ponies, are prized for their tough, hard feet.

Poor foot quality may be caused by poor nutrition. If a pony lacks essential nutrients, he will probably not be able to grow healthy feet—or, come to that, healthy skin and hair.

From the front, the cannon bone of each foreleg should come straight down from the centre of the knee and the feet should not turn in or out. Any deviation puts extra strain on limbs and feet and affects the straightness of the pony's movement.

Being 'over at the knee' and 'back at the knee' are common foreleg faults. If the outline between the bottom of the knee and the top of the fetlock is convex, the pony is over at the knee; if it is concave, he is back at the knee. Being back at the knee is more of a problem, as it puts strain on the tendons.

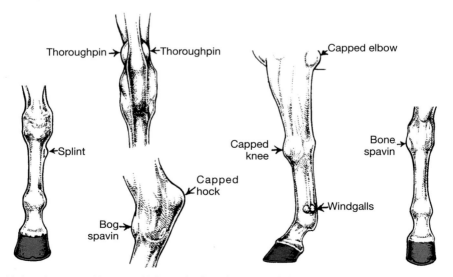

Various lumps and bumps which can be found on a pony's legs.

Pasterns should have a reasonable but not exaggerated length and slope to help absorb concussion and give a comfortable ride. The angle usually mirrors that of the shoulder, so a pony with an upright shoulder will usually have upright pasterns.

Hind leg conformation is important because it is from here and the hindquarters that power is generated. Hock joints do a lot of work and the weakest kind of hock is the sickle hock, where the leg comes in front of an imaginary perpendicular line dropped from the point of the hock to the ground.

Cow hocks, where the hocks turn inwards, are a more common defect and again, can be a sign of weakness. However, they do not usually cause a problem unless pronounced. If the angle of the hock is too wide, the hind leg will be too straight, which is also a sign of weakness.

Lumps and bumps

While it is good to see clean limbs—ones that are unblemished—blemishes do not always affect soundness. However, if they are related to poor conformation, they are a sign that the structure is under strain. A vet will discuss their significance with you during a pre-purchase examination. Many blemishes are detrimental to a show pony, but not necessarily to others, though lumps and bumps associated with arthritic changes to joints obviously signify that the pony has a problem.

The commonest blemishes are splints, bony enlargements on the inside of the leg that are commonly caused either by concussion or by a blow to the limb. Once they are formed, they rarely cause problems, unless they are in a position where they interfere with the knee joint. They are usually found on the forelegs, though they may also develop on the hind ones.

You may also see windgalls, soft but not painful swellings in the fetlock or tendon areas. Again, these rarely cause a problem.

Capped hocks or elbows, where fluid distends the point of the hock or the elbow, are unsightly but do not affect soundness. They are often caused by a pony scraping himself on a hard concrete floor, either because he has insufficient bedding or because he has dug a hole in his bed.

A curb, which is a swelling on the back of the hind leg just below the hock, is usually associated with poor conformation and as such, is frowned upon. However, some animals have curbs on both hind legs and never seem to be affected by them.

Thoroughpins and bog spavins are soft swellings seen in the hock area and while they rarely cause lameness, are often associated with poor conformation and as such, highlight a potential problem. Thoroughpins occur just above the point of the hock and bog spavins develop just below it.

Do not confuse a bog spavin with a bone spavin. The latter is related to degenerative joint disease of the hock and in some cases, there may be no outward visible sign.

While you need to recognise blemishes, do not panic and assume that a pony with a blemish is automatically unsuitable. The only way to determine whether or not a blemish is significant is to ask your vet's advice when a pre-purchase vetting is carried out (see Chapter 7). One school of thought says that a pony who has been in regular work for several years and not acquired a lump, bump or scar has never done a 'proper' day's work. That is not necessarily true, but there are many ponies with blemished limbs who are as sound and as tough as the proverbial old boot.

The front end

In general, it does not matter whether a pony's head is pretty or plain, but because he uses his head and neck to balance, they should look as if they belong together. If a pony has a big head, he will find it easier to balance if his neck is shorter rather than longer.

It is often said that a small eye is a sign of a mean temperament, but although a large eye is more attractive, this is not true. Similarly, a pony's vision and temperament will not be affected if he has blue or wall eyes, or if you can see the sclera (white ring) all the way round one or both eyes.

If you enjoy doing makeovers, remember that the right bridle can make the most of any pony's head. A technically plain head can look stunning in a bridle with a wider noseband than would suit a finer, prettier head.

The angle at which the head joins the neck should not be too sharp, or the pony will find it difficult to flex. Another important connection is that of the neck to the withers. If the neck is set on too low, the pony will naturally go with a lower head carriage than English-style riders would want.

You do not want a pony to have a ewe neck, which looks as if it has been attached upside down. It takes an experienced eye to tell the difference between a true (skeletally) ewe neck and a basically correct neck structure where, because of incorrect riding and training, muscle has been built up underneath rather than on top.

The shape of the withers only causes difficulties if it is exaggeratedly high or, as is the case with many ponies and cobs, barely defined. This is not because it has an effect on soundness, but because defined withers make it easier to fit a saddle and more likely that it will stay in place. A good saddle fitter will be able to help even if you have a pony with prominent withers or a flat withers profile.

The shape of the shoulder is much more important, as it defines the way the pony is able to move his forelegs. If the angle of the shoulder blade is too sharp and upright, he will have an up and down stride, particularly noticeable in trot. You may hear this described as a 'sewing machine trot' because it mimics the angle of a sewing machine needle. If the shoulder is well-sloped, the stride will go forwards rather than up and down. This will make the pony more comfortable to ride. It will also mean that there is less concussion on his limbs and feet, so can be a factor in him staying sound.

From the front, a pony should have enough width through the chest to ensure that his forelegs are not too close together. If they are, a fault which is sometimes described as 'having both legs coming out of the same hole', he is more likely to knock one limb against the other.

On the other hand, a pony who is excessively wide in the chest is likely to have a rolling gait that will make him uncomfortable to ride.

Left: Correct neck conformation and **(right)** ewe neck.

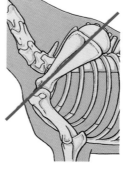

The anatomy of **(left)** a correctly-angled shoulder and **(right)** an upright shoulder.

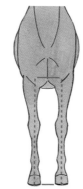

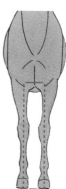

From left to right: A chest with correct conformation; a chest which is too wide; a chest which is too narrow.

In the middle

A pony needs to be deep enough through the girth to allow sufficient room for his heart and lungs to function efficiently. Do not confuse this with being fat. You should still be able to feel his ribs, even if you have to press your hand against him slightly.

The bottom line of his belly should not curve upwards sharply. This fault is known as being herring-gutted, because it mimics the shape of that fish.

A horse who is herring-gutted will always look like a greyhound and is said to be 'run up light'. With this sort of conformation, saddles tend to slip back, but a good saddle fitter will be able to help.

Racehorses and three-day-event horses who are at maximum fitness may at first glance appear to be herring-gutted, but if you look more closely, you will see that they are actually lean and toned. Horses in this condition are sometimes also described as 'running up light'.

The profile and length of a pony's back should be taken into consideration. It should have a curve, but not a pronounced dip, though old ponies who are no longer worked often develop dipped backs as they lose muscle tone.

A dipped (sway) back which is a result of skeletal conformation is a sign of weakness, though what appears to be a weak back can actually be at least partly a consequence of lack of tone in the abdominal muscles. To lift his back, a horse has to lift his abdomen.

The opposite fault is a roach back, with a convex rather than a slightly concave outline. Some riders believe that both a roach back and a completely straight back may give a tendency to stiffness, but the influence and importance of the abdominal muscles is such that these faults tend to be less of a problem than a dipped back.

A long-backed animal is often comfortable to ride, but a back which is markedly long is a sign of weakness and also makes it harder for the animal to 'step under' fully with his hind legs and thus balance himself. Mares are usually slightly longer in the back than geldings. This is a natural conformation point and as long as it is not exaggerated, is not a fault, as it allows room for a mare to carry a foal.

A short back is, in general, stronger than a long one. However, if it is too short, it may cause problems with saddle fit—though they should not be insurmountable. Because the distance between the forelegs and hind legs is also relatively short, a short-backed animal may be more likely to strike into the back of a front heel or leg with the toe of a hind one.

From top to bottom: Long back; short back; dipped back; roach back.

The back end

The hindquarters, together with the hind legs, are very important, as they supply the pony's pushing power. If a pony were a car, his engine would be at the back.

It can be easy to confuse a weak back end with one that lacks muscle. Muscle development only comes through correct work. Look at the length from hip to hock; if it is noticeably short, this is a sign of weakness. Do not confuse the round hindquarters of an overweight pony with strength.

Although young ponies who are still growing go through stages where the back end is higher than the front, a mature animal who is croup-high will tend to go on his forehand because he is built 'downhill'. Unless the fault is exaggerated, it can usually be overcome by correct schooling.

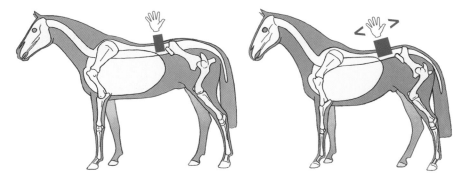

Left: The skeleton of a horse with correct barrel conformation, showing a hand's width between the last rib and the point of the hip.

Right: In a herring-gutted horse, the distance between the last rib and the point of the hip is greater than a hand's width.

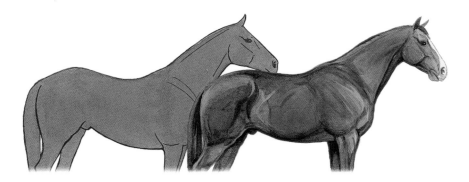

Left: A horse with a high croup.

Right: A horse with a correct top line—a series of gentle curves running smoothly into each other.

Movement

Conformation and movement go together. The best scenario is always that a pony moves straight—in other words, his limbs and feet follow the most efficient flight path, without swinging to one side or the other. Straight movement means that the concussion which has to be absorbed every time the pony takes a step results in less strain on all the structures that make up the feet and limbs. It also means that the pony is less likely to knock one leg with another limb or foot.

To assess the true quality of a pony's movement, you need to see him led out on a loose rein or lead rope, first in walk, then in trot. Watch from the front, from behind, and from each side in turn.

A pony who throws out one or both forefeet is said to dish, whereas putting one forefoot in front of the other is called plaiting. Brushing, which is when the pony knocks one leg against the other, can cause injury.

Forging, where the toe of a hind shoe strikes the sole of a forefoot or the heel of a front shoe, may be caused by lack of balance—perhaps because a rider makes a pony trot too quickly—or by weakness. Overreaching is another form of contact between a hind foot and a forefoot, but in this case the hind foot impacts on the heel or the back of the pastern.

Some ponies move too close behind and will brush one hind leg against the other, often in the fetlock area. Again, causes include poor conformation or lack of balance. Younger animals who have not yet muscled up may do this until they are more developed.

Protective boots and regular attention from a good farrier can minimise the risk of injury from imperfect movement. In most cases, unless you are aiming to take the show ring by storm, you only need to worry if the fault is marked. There are many dressage stars who look less than perfect heading up the centre line!

Protective boots can minimise the risk of injury, though many riders use them as standard.

6. Viewing and Trying

You should now be ready to look at and try potential partners, so all your research and preparation can be put to good use. If you are inexperienced, it is a good idea to get a knowledgeable adult to help you, though make sure you ask someone who really does fit that description. While a young rider's opinion and input is important, children should never be allowed to make such decisions by themselves.

A professional adviser such as an instructor will probably expect to be paid for time spent with you, which is perfectly reasonable. However, they should not advise on a purchase in which they have a financial interest, or be paid a 'recommendation fee' by a seller.

Whether or not you take an adviser with you for a first viewing, or look at a pony first and get an expert eye on a return visit, is up to you. A compromise may be to take photographs and a short video of a pony to show your adviser, but do not do this without asking the seller's permission first. If parents do not want you to film their children, you have to respect that, but you can still ask to take a short clip of the pony standing, walking and trotting in hand.

There are times when a knowledgeable buyer will see a horse or pony once and know that he is the right animal for the job. In most cases, though, be prepared to look at a pony twice, even if the seller tells you that there is a list of people waiting to look at him. That may be true, but a second look is often a good idea.

Although buying a pony is a big step to take, do not expect to make so many visits that the yard owner allocates you a parking space. Any seller should be prepared for you to see the pony twice, but to expect more than that is, perhaps, asking a bit much. The exception may be the seller who is so determined to find the perfect home that you find yourself being inspected just as much as you are inspecting the pony!

First Impressions

Hopefully, seeing photographs and/or a video of a pony will mean that your first impression of him will be positive. Most people will have the pony waiting in a stable, unless he lives out all the time. This means that he should be clean and dry. You can't assess a pony's feet and limbs if they are plastered in mud, so the seller should at least have ensured that he is reasonably clean.

Opposite: Whorls are distinctive and individual and can be used as part of the identification process by a vet.

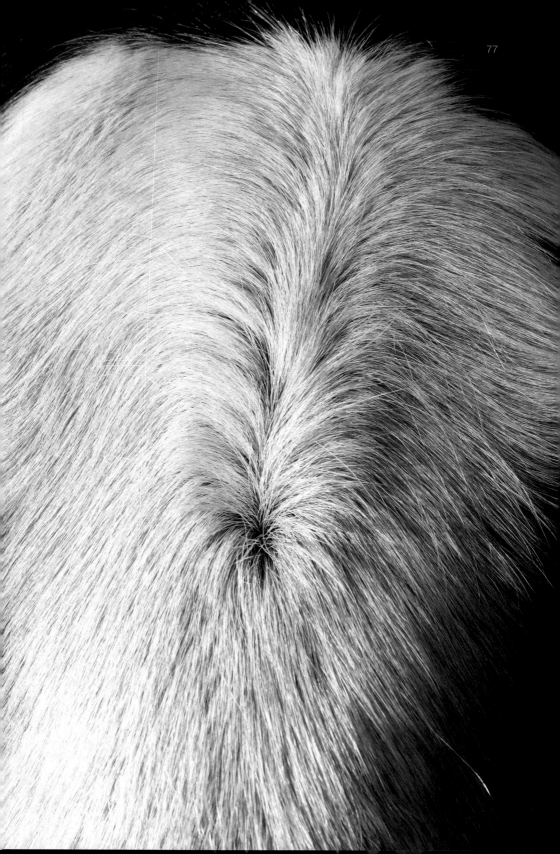

A pony who is happy in his environment will also be relaxed. A relaxed pony will not have the charisma of one who is alert and interested, so it is not necessarily a bad thing if he is resting a hind leg or looks rather dozy. On the other hand, if he looks as if he is poised for flight or lays back his ears as soon as you approach him, start making your excuses to leave!

Always watch the seller go into the stable first to gauge the pony's reaction. The pony should be amenable to having a headcollar put on and, if he is wearing a rug, to having it removed.

If he seems quiet to handle, approach him calmly and let him get used to you. Do not let an excited child rush up to a pony, no matter how quiet the pony seems. Without pretending to be more knowledgeable than you are, run your hand down his neck and shoulder and ask if you can pick up his feet.

Remember not to grab or poke at him, but to be calm, clear and polite. Hopefully, he will also have been taught to back up and move over in the stable in response to hand pressure.

If all goes well, his potential rider can meet him and the seller can bring the pony out of the stable for you. At some stage, you should be offered his passport to inspect. If not, ask to see it. In many cases, you will be able to see from the identification section that it is likely to be the correct one, but if the pony is a bay with two white socks and a solid-coloured head and the passport shows a bay with three white socks and a white star (small patch) on his head, the documentation does not belong to this pony.

If a pony has a solid coat colour and no white markings, he can be identified by the whorls in his coat, small patches of hair growing in a circular pattern. Every horse and pony has a unique set of whorls and a vet will compare and hopefully match them to the description in the passport as part of a pre-purchase identification.

TIP

Pretending to know more than you do will only make you look silly. It is not worth looking in a pony's mouth to assess his age unless you know what you are looking at. In any case, ageing by dentition is much harder once a pony has a full set of adult teeth at five years and in most cases—and certainly in that of a first pony for a novice rider—you will be buying an older animal. Although there are markers to look for, such as hooks which usually appear on the corner teeth when a pony is seven years old, they are not totally reliable.

Assessing Conformation and Movement

You need to see the pony standing on level ground to get an accurate picture. Follow the guidelines in the previous chapter and, if you are a novice buyer making a first visit, be honest—try to get a general impression, but explain that you would want to return with an adviser if you decided the pony might be the one for you.

Take the same approach to assessing the pony's movement, but try to make sure he is not lame. Unless it is really severe, lameness shows in trot rather than in walk and it is easier to recognise lameness in a foreleg than in a hind leg. Mild lameness, especially in a hind leg, may only be recognised by someone who is very experienced and sometimes, only by a vet.

If you are buying privately, do you get the impression that the pony has been looked after well and that it is important to the seller that he finds the right home? It is not a good sign if the pony is grossly fat or underweight, or if his shoes have been on for so long that they are paper thin and are coming loose.

Some people believe that if a pony is newly shod, it is a seller's ploy to disguise problems. Being cautious is one thing, but being overly suspicious is another, especially if you have done your research. As you look at the pony, you may want to ask questions you did not raise on your initial enquiry.

Listening is just as important as asking, as more information can often be picked up during conversation.

If you see anything which makes you realise that the pony is definitely not the one for you, say so now. It is rude and unfair to criticise a pony, even if he does have the worst cow hocks, biggest splints and most exaggerated sway back you have ever seen. A simple 'Thank you, but he isn't quite what we are looking for', is clear and polite and saves everyone's time.

Seeing the pony ridden

If you like what you have seen, ask to see the pony ridden. Never let a child try a pony before someone else has ridden him to show you how he behaves, no matter how quiet he is said to be. It is not just that, if a pony is going to misbehave, you want to see it happen with someone else. You may find that although he is well behaved and well schooled, he is obviously too forward-going or sensitive for his intended new rider.

In this case, again, it is better to say what a lovely pony he is, but that he would be too much for your child at this stage. If you are not sure, but your child is keen to try him, ask if you can come back with your adviser and get a knowledgeable opinion on whether the rider is ready for the pony. Never push a child who does not feel ready to ride a particular pony, as you risk damaging the child's confidence. It is unfair on the pony, too.

The seller should arrange for you to see the pony ridden in all gaits in a safe environment. If it is intended that the pony will be jumped, this should also be demonstrated to you. You can learn a lot by watching, and things to notice include:

- Is the pony wearing simple tack? You would hope to see a pony for a novice rider wearing a simple snaffle bridle, not a potentially more severe bit.
- Does he stand quietly while the rider mounts? It is reasonable for an adult to stand at a pony's head, but not to have to hang on to it.
- Does the pony wait for the rider's commands, or try to rush off as soon as he gets the chance?
- When he is asked to go to the school or area where the rider will show him off to you, does he go willingly, or hang back?
- Is he happy to go on both reins (clockwise and anticlockwise) or is he noticeably more reluctant or resistant on one than the other?
- Does he hang or duck towards the gate?
- If he is asked to jump, is he calm and willing and happy to jump both going away from and towards home?
- When he has cantered and jumped, does he stay relaxed, or seem more excited?

Trying for Yourself

If your impressions are generally favourable and you have not seen anything that makes you feel the pony would be beyond your child's capability, it is time for a test ride. Make sure that the rider does not feel under pressure and is given plenty of time to adjust stirrup leathers and reins to a suitable length and to get used to the feel of the pony.

A child who has been used to familiar ponies at a riding school, or needs a bigger pony to replace one who has been outgrown, may be slightly nervous, even if normally confident. While some sellers can be pleasant and encouraging and give a child every chance to get used to a pony, others may—even if with the best of intentions—be rather intimidating. It is also nerve-racking for a child to ride a pony in front of his previous and perhaps critical rider, especially if the pony is a much-loved member of the family!

The pony should be tried at all gaits in safe surroundings. If appropriate, this should include jumping, though a less experienced buyer should not feel pushed to try to ride at the same level as the current owner. In some cases, especially if a child lacks confidence, it may be better to leave riding the pony at faster gaits and jumping until you return with your adviser/instructor.

A seller will want to show you what the pony is capable of, whether that is a first pony who stands like a rock while a child mounts from one side and dismounts on the other, or a star member of The Pony Club Branch teams who makes light of a course of decent-sized fences. Someone who, for instance, is trying the latter pony with a view to gaining experience and eventually moving up the competition levels will be happier and safer tackling a smaller course.

Trying a pony in open spaces, when appropriate, will help you decide if he is suitable.

Open spaces and open roads

While it is often advisable to start off seeing a pony ridden in an arena, if possible—and for a child to try him in a safe, enclosed area—you need to make sure that he is happy and safe when worked in an open space. If he is said to be suitable for hacking, you will also need confirmation of this.

While an experienced rider will be capable of hacking out a horse or pony with a competent escort, and will expect to do so, this may not be appropriate or safe in all cases. If in doubt, wait until you return with an adviser and assess the situation then.

You could, perhaps, ask to see the pony hacked out and follow at a safe distance. This is not as satisfactory, but is safer than expecting an inexperienced child to cope on a pony he or she does not know.

Do not expect the seller to allow the pony to be hacked out alone, even if the rider is experienced and at The Pony Club's upper age limit. Put yourself in the seller's position: would you allow a total stranger to ride off alone on your pony?

If you intend the pony to be tried out hacking, the rider who is thinking of buying him should wear high-viz gear even if the escort chooses not to. Be seen and be safe is more than just a cliché.

TIPS FOR EXPERIENCED RIDERS

An experienced rider can tell a lot about a horse or pony by the way he behaves out hacking. Things you may wish to try include:

- As you do not know the pony, start off behind your escort. When appropriate and in safe surroundings, ride alongside—first on the inside, then on the outside.
- If all goes well, ask to take the lead to make sure the pony will do so.
- Although this may not always be possible, it is useful to be able to canter in a safe area. Again, it is helpful to be able to try the pony behind and in front of the escort.
- Most horses and ponies know when they are heading for home. While the pony may seem more willing to walk out going home, one who starts jogging or pulling will not be an enjoyable ride and although it may be possible to improve such behaviour, it can be difficult to do so.
- When you get back to the yard, make sure you are in front and ask the pony to walk past the entrance. Warn the escort that you are going to do this. It's natural for a pony to hesitate, as he will know he has reached home and will not understand why he is being asked to go away from it, but he should still walk past when given clear aids.

Trial periods

Many people will advise you that you should not buy a pony without arranging to have him on trial for a week or two, but while some sellers will agree to this, especially in the case of a first pony, others will not.

If you are able to take him on trial, it is important to have a written agreement detailing responsibilities of both sides. Is the pony insured for veterinary fees and, if not, who is responsible for any incurred if he is injured or becomes ill? Do the owners have public liability insurance that covers you as well as them? It might seem as if you are causing unnecessary complications and hopefully, nothing will go wrong—but if it does, you do not want the situation to be made worse because of disagreements over who is liable or responsible.

Do not be suspicious of sellers who refuse a trial period, especially if the pony is well-schooled and valuable. Again, put yourself in their position. However, if the seller lives locally and realises that you are a genuine buyer, you may be able to arrange to visit and try the pony under their supervision for a short period. This will enable you to get to know him and for the seller to get to know you and, if all goes well, will make the transition to a new home less nerve-racking for all concerned.

Any trial period should be looked on as a chance to double-check that the pony you have set your heart on is suitable for the rider, and vice versa. It is not a strategy to decide whether a pony you are not sure about might turn out to be suitable, or a practice run to make sure that you are ready to buy.

The One for You

Eventually, you will find the pony who seems ideal. The next step is to agree on a price, whether you are completing the purchase immediately or having the pony on trial. Put everything in writing, to avoid any misunderstandings or even gazumpings. It has been known for sellers to up the price when they know a buyer has fallen in love with a pony who has been on trial and for buyers to try to haggle the price down at the end of a trial period.

The price is right

In many—but not all—cases, sellers are prepared to negotiate on price and some may advertise the pony at a slightly higher price than they are prepared to accept, so take this into account. If you feel uncomfortable trying to negotiate, ask your adviser to do so on your behalf.

However, some people will state a 'take it or leave it' price and you will have to do just that, though you may be able to come to an arrangement about the pony's tack and/or rugs and other equipment. It is only worth having these if they fit the pony well and are in good condition, so a novice owner will need to get advice.

It is recommended that you ask a specialist equine vet to carry out a pre-purchase examination before you pay for the pony. This is explained in the next section. Some people may feel this is unnecessary if you are buying an old pony who will not work hard and is not worth a lot in financial terms, but only a vet can tell if, for instance, a pony has a heart problem or an eyesight defect. Either could put the rider's safety at risk. There is also the point that if you buy a pony who turns out to be unsuitable because of an existing health problem, you will have to deal with disappointment and expense.

Once you have agreed a price, be prepared to pay a deposit and get a written receipt. Some sellers will ask for a token sum, but professional sellers may often require 10 per cent of the purchase price to deter buyers who agree to buy a pony then change their minds. Either way, get a written agreement of the sum paid, the fact that it is refundable if the pony fails a pre-purchase vetting, and the final amount payable.

Many years ago, horses and ponies would be sold on the basis of a handshake. Today, we live in a litigious world and it really is best to get everything in writing, even if you are buying from a friend. Misunderstandings can arise and it's better to have an agreement than risk losing a friendship. Anyone who is offended by this should, on reflection, realise that a written agreement protects both buyer and seller.

Which vet?

If you buy a pony locally, it should be easy to find a good equine vet to carry out a pre-purchase examination. Ask your instructor or adviser to recommend a practice. The only problem you may encounter is if the seller is a client of the vet you want to instruct. Some vets will feel it is unwise to vet a pony belonging to an existing client, while others will be happy to do so on the basis that the seller agrees that the pony's full medical history is disclosed. The latter scenario has to be a bonus for the buyer, but if the vet is unwilling to carry out an examination it does not necessarily mean that the pony has had anything other than the usual preventive treatment.

If you know a good local vet and buy a pony further afield, you either have to ask the vet to travel—which will add considerably to the expense—or ask a practice in that area to do the job. A vet in your area may know and recommend a practice, or you can find ones in that area via the Royal College of Veterinary Surgeons, which has a search facility on its website.

Fit for the job

When you arrange a vetting—and you should book this as soon as possible after you have agreed a deal—be honest about the purpose for which the pony will be used. It is fine to dream of glory at The Pony Club Championships, but if the reality is that you want to buy a first or second pony to have fun with at Pony Club rallies and low key competitions, do not exaggerate.

When a vetting is carried out, it is to establish that there are no clinical signs of injury or illness that will preclude a pony being used for a particular purpose. As the demands on a top level competition pony are higher than those on one used for less strenuous activities, you may find that by exaggerating, you miss out on the perfect pony.

A vetting is not a warranty, but a professional opinion. It is not a guarantee that the pony will never suffer problems, nor should the vet be concerned about the price being paid, or the rider's ability.

The vetting follows a set format and afterwards, the vet will explain his or her findings. If a problem appears early on which makes it obvious that the pony is not suitable for your purpose, the vetting will stop at that point.

As mentioned, there will never be a perfect pony, so expect a list of pluses and minuses. Once these have been explained to you—either in person, if you are there when it is carried out, or by telephone afterwards—the vet will make a recommendation as to whether or not you should buy the pony. If the report is unfavourable, it is up to you whether or not you take that advice, but you will ignore it at your peril.

Investigating insurance

Insurance is explained in more detail in the next chapter but, if you have not already looked into it, now is the time to be thinking about whether or not you are going to insure your new pony and what you are going to cover. Although companies will not give you specific quotes until you can give exact details of the animal to be insured, it is worth doing some initial groundwork, so that you do not rush to accept unsuitable cover when you suddenly find yourself the owner of a pony.

7. Getting Him Home

Finalising Insurance

When the vet has given the recommendation to purchase, you will need to pay the balance of the price and arrange transport. As soon as payment is made, the pony becomes your property so, if possible, arrange insurance before taking him to his new home. Cover can usually be arranged over the telephone and the insurers will then send you the necessary documentation.

As a member of The Pony Club, you automatically get public liability insurance, which is something no horse or pony owner can afford to be without. It is also recommended that you arrange cover for veterinary fees. Diagnostic and treatment options have become increasingly sophisticated and, inevitably, increasingly expensive. Remember that whether the patient is a racehorse worth millions or a family pony worth a few hundred pounds, the costs will be the same—and, of course, every animal deserves the best treatment regardless of financial value.

Some insurance policies offer various forms of cover in a blanket policy while others allow you to mix and match options. The latter is often best; for instance, there is no point in paying for public liability insurance when you already have this through The Pony Club.

You will need to have lessons with your horse or pony to build up a relationship and progress.

Facts and figures

Mortality cover, which is paid out if a pony dies or has to be put down on the advice of a vet, is standard on all policies. Your pony will be insured for the purchase price or his market value, whatever is the lower, but if an insurance company agrees to insure your pony for the purchase price, it should accept that this is his market value.

Veterinary fees cover is optional on most policies but, for most owners, this is an important form of insurance. Different companies offer different amounts of cover, but it is easy to run up bills of thousands of pounds if a pony needs lengthy treatment or surgery.

Loss of use cover is an expensive option and means that all—or, more usually, part—of the sum insured will be paid out if, because of injury, or other health issues, the pony can no longer be used for activities for which he is insured.

You may want to insure your saddlery and tack. Before opting for this as part of your equine insurance policy, check whether or not you are covered on your household contents insurance. If this seems to be the case, double-check the policy to make sure that the tack is covered if kept elsewhere other than at home.

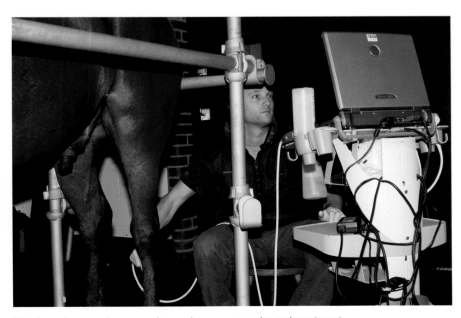

Veterinary fees can be expensive, so insurance can be an investment.

Points to remember

- Ask friends about their experiences of insurance companies. While it's a bonus if some names get consistently good recommendations, those made by owners who have made claims are usually more useful.
- All decisions relating to the payment of veterinary fee cover are dependent on a written explanation and recommendation by your vet.
- All policies include an excess. This is the amount paid by you towards any sum claimed, and will vary. Some companies give you the option of paying a higher excess in return for a lower annual premium.
- Your policy will not cover a pre-existing condition. For instance, if you buy a pony with a condition that does not affect his use, but causes problems later on, the insurers will be unlikely to pay for treatment.
- Insurance companies are unlikely to insure any animal who has previously been the subject of a loss of use claim.
- As soon as you get your insurance documents, read them thoroughly. If you do not understand anything, ring up the company and ask.
- Some companies offer cover from the day the policy is taken out. Others specify that cover will not apply for a short period, usually ten to fourteen days.

On the Move

Sometimes, a seller will be prepared to transport a pony to his new home. If not, and if you do not have your own transport, you will need to arrange for someone to do it for you. An experienced friend may offer to fetch a pony who has been bought locally, but if there is any element of hire or reward, you may run into problems relating to transport legislation.

Similarly, if you have bought a trailer or horsebox in anticipation of owning a pony, first get plenty of practice towing or driving in safe surroundings, without a pony on board. Ideally, get lessons from a professional driving instructor who specialises in this area.

Anyone who intends to tow a horse trailer in the UK and passed a driving test after 1 January 1997 must pass the official trailer towing test before doing so. In the case of horseboxes, check that you hold the correct driving licence for the weight of the vehicle you intend to drive.

Home, Sweet Home

Settling in

If you are keeping your new pony at a livery yard, the owner should have a system in place for settling in new arrivals. Try to arrange for the pony to arrive in daylight at a quiet time on the yard so that he can take in his new surroundings.

Some yards, especially those that house competition animals, will insist that new occupants are kept in a form of quarantine for a short time to ensure that any incubating problems not picked up on a vetting are not passed on to others. No one wants to bring in problems, whether minor or more severe.

Other yards will not impose these conditions, especially if the pony is known to them and the vet has given an all-clear. However, he still needs to be introduced to his new home carefully. Ideally, when he is turned out for the first time it should be in a small paddock with a quiet companion. Once he has settled, he can be turned out with others.

Horses and ponies who are turned out together regularly form a natural pecking order and your pony will have to find his place in this. Some ponies are naturally dominant and some naturally subservient and the only way to find out how yours will behave is to wait and watch.

At first, he may be chased off and you will see him grazing apart from the others, but eventually he will make friends with another pony in the group and find his place within it. Alternatively, he may be a bossy pony who tries to exert his authority from day one. How well or otherwise this goes down

Towing a trailer safely takes practice and you must comply with legal requirements.

will depend on the others in the group, but it is usually best to let ponies sort things out amongst themselves.

Occasionally, you may find that a pony who was guaranteed not to exhibit stereotypical behaviour does just that when stabled at his new home. He may stop when he settles in, but it is sensible to inform the seller that he is doing this and, if necessary, to set a time limit, after which you may want to return him or negotiate a return of part of the purchase price. Unless you have bought him from a professional seller and have full protection under the Sale of Goods Act, this may not always be easy.

A new regime

Before your pony leaves his old home, you should double check the information about his regime. When extra forage is needed, does he get hay or haylage? If he gets extra hard feed, what type and brand is it, how much does he get and how often is he fed? How often is he ridden and what is his workload?

One of the biggest mistakes people make is to overfeed a new purchase. They then find that he has too much energy and is difficult to ride. If he has been given hard feed, it is far better to cut back the amount or even cut it out, then gradually add or increase it. You have to accept that any pony, no matter how naturally quiet his temperament and no matter how well behaved, will be uncertain of new surroundings and new people.

It will take a few days for your pony to start to get used to his new home. Some settle more quickly than others and if you can follow a regime that, as far as possible, mirrors the one he is used to, this will help.

Building a relationship with a pony is like building one with a person. You do not become best friends in a matter of days: it takes time to build mutual confidence. While it is usually a good idea to start working your pony after he has been at the yard a day or two, take things gradually, even though you will be eager to start doing things with him.

Before you ride him for the first time, it might be sensible to lunge him or, if you are not confident about doing this, ask your instructor or another competent adult to do so. If you have the facilities available, ride in an arena. Keep things simple and think about establishing communication: at this stage, you are getting to know each other. Some riders feel happier if they have the support of an instructor they are used to for this first ride.

When you are ready for your first hack, go out with a sensible rider on a sensible horse or pony, not someone who will want to canter at every opportunity. It is better to stick to walk and trot for the first few rides out.

Making progress

As your relationship with your pony develops, you will both gain in confidence. Soon you will be ready to enjoy all sorts of activities, including Pony Club rallies and competitions. It is important to carry on having lessons, because that will help you make progress and avoid problems.

There will be times when things do not go exactly according to plan. You might hit a setback in your schooling, or find that your pony has or develops a behavioural quirk. Never ignore minor problems, because left unattended, they grow into bigger ones. However, they are often down to a glitch in communication and, with the right help, you will be able to sort them out and progress.

Make sure you only take advice from people you respect. There may be other owners who give you conflicting advice, but even though they may mean well, it is better to stick with those whose knowledge and experience you are sure of.

As a member of The Pony Club, you will never be far from a reliable source of knowledge. You will also have plenty of fun—so enjoy your pony!

As you get to know your new partner, you'll be able to enjoy all sorts of activities.

Index

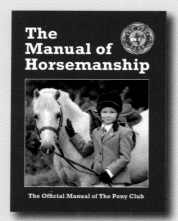
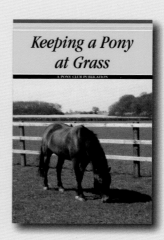